# Transitions and Animations in CSS

*Adding Motion with CSS*

*Estelle Weyl*

Beijing · Boston · Farnham · Sebastopol · Tokyo

**Transitions and Animations in CSS**

by Estelle Weyl

Printed in the United States of America.

Published by O'Reilly Media, Inc., 1005 Gravenstein Highway North, Sebastopol, CA 95472.

O'Reilly books may be purchased for educational, business, or sales promotional use. Online editions are also available for most titles (*http://safaribooksonline.com*). For more information, contact our corporate/institutional sales department: 800-998-9938 or *corporate@oreilly.com*.

| | |
|---|---|
| **Editor:** Meg Foley | **Interior Designer:** David Futato |
| **Production Editor:** Colleen Lobner | **Cover Designer:** Randy Comer |
| **Copyeditor:** Molly Ives Brower | **Illustrator:** Rebecca Demarest |
| **Proofreader:** Amanda Kersey | |

May 2016:          First Edition

**Revision History for the First Edition**
2016-04-12:    First Release

See *http://oreilly.com/catalog/errata.csp?isbn=9781491929889* for release details.

978-1-491-92988-9

[LSI]

# Table of Contents

# Preface

## Conventions Used in This Book

The following typographical conventions are used in this book:

*Italic*
> Indicates new terms, URLs, email addresses, filenames, and file extensions.

`Constant width`
> Used for program listings, as well as within paragraphs to refer to program elements such as variable or function names, databases, data types, environment variables, statements, and keywords.

**`Constant width bold`**
> Shows commands or other text that should be typed literally by the user.

*`Constant width italic`*
> Shows text that should be replaced with user-supplied values or by values determined by context.

 This element signifies a general note.

## Using Code Examples

Whenever you come across an icon that looks like ⊙, it means there is an associated code example. Live examples are available at *http://standardista.com/css3/transitions* and *http://standardista.com/css3/animations*. You can either click on the ⊙ icon while reading this book in electronic format to go directly to a live version of the code example referenced, or visit those links for a list of all of the code examples found in the Transitions and Animations chapters.

This book is here to help you get your job done. In general, if example code is offered with this book, you may use it in your programs and documentation. You do not need to contact us for permission unless you're reproducing a significant portion of the code. For example, writing a program that uses several chunks of code from this book does not require permission. Selling or distributing a CD-ROM of examples from O'Reilly books does require permission. Answering a question by citing this book and quoting example code does not require permission. Incorporating a significant amount of example code from this book into your product's documentation does require permission.

We appreciate, but do not require, attribution. An attribution usually includes the title, author, publisher, and ISBN. For example: "*Transitions and Animations in CSS* by Estelle Weyl (O'Reilly). Copyright 2016 Estelle Weyl, 978-1-4919-2988-9."

If you feel your use of code examples falls outside fair use or the permission given above, feel free to contact us at *permissions@oreilly.com*.

## Safari® Books Online

 *Safari Books Online* is an on-demand digital library that delivers expert content in both book and video form from the world's leading authors in technology and business.

Technology professionals, software developers, web designers, and business and creative professionals use Safari Books Online as their primary resource for research, problem solving, learning, and certification training.

Safari Books Online offers a range of plans and pricing for enterprise, government, education, and individuals.

Members have access to thousands of books, training videos, and prepublication manuscripts in one fully searchable database from publishers like O'Reilly Media, Prentice Hall Professional, Addison-Wesley Professional, Microsoft Press, Sams, Que, Peachpit Press, Focal Press, Cisco Press, John Wiley & Sons, Syngress, Morgan Kaufmann, IBM Redbooks, Packt, Adobe Press, FT Press, Apress, Manning, New Riders, McGraw-Hill, Jones & Bartlett, Course Technology, and hundreds more. For more information about Safari Books Online, please visit us online.

# How to Contact Us

Please address comments and questions concerning this book to the publisher:

O'Reilly Media, Inc.
1005 Gravenstein Highway North
Sebastopol, CA 95472
800-998-9938 (in the United States or Canada)
707-829-0515 (international or local)
707-829-0104 (fax)

We have a web page for this book, where we list errata and any additional information. You can access this page at *http://bit.ly/transitions-and-animations-in-css*.

To comment or ask technical questions about this book, send email to *bookquestions@oreilly.com*.

For more information about our books, courses, conferences, and news, see our website at *http://www.oreilly.com*.

Find us on Facebook: *http://facebook.com/oreilly*

Follow us on Twitter: *http://twitter.com/oreillymedia*

Watch us on YouTube: *http://www.youtube.com/oreillymedia*

You can also find Estelle Weyl on Twitter at *@estellevw*, *@standardista*, and *@webdevtips*.

# Acknowledgments

Thank you to the technical reviewers:

Matt Rakow is a program manager at Microsoft, working on the Internet Explorer and Edge browsers since 2010 and the W3C CSS Working Group since 2013. His current focus is advancing the capability and performance of webpage composition and rendering, but also is devoted to improving scrolling performance, touch interactions, and high pixel density screen support.

David Baron is a distinguished engineer at Mozilla. He's been involved in the CSS community and the development of the Gecko layout engine since 1998. At Mozilla, Baron implemented media queries, CSS transitions and animations, and the CSS `calc()` function, and designed and implemented the reftest test format and fixes for `:visited` privacy. As a participant at the W3C, he has edited the CSS Color Module, CSS Conditional Rules, CSS Transitions, CSS Animations, and the CSS Overflow

Module. He can be found on Twitter at *@davidbaron*, and on the Web (*http://dbaron.org*).

Sarah Drasner is an award-winning Senior UX Engineer at Trulia (Zillow Group). She is also a staff writer at CSS-Tricks. She has worked for 15 years as a web developer and designer, and at points worked concurrently as a scientific illustrator and a college professor. Sarah loves SVG, informative animation, and welding together pieces of the DOM. Follow her at *@sarah_edo*, on CodePen (*http://codepen.io/sdras*), or her website (*http://sarahdrasnerdesign.com*).

# CHAPTER 1

# CSS Transitions and Animations

CSS transforms, CSS transitions, and CSS animations are three separate CSS specifications. While the three terms sound like they may do the same thing—make something move—CSS transitions and animations make things move *over time*. Transitions and animations let you define the transition between two or more states of an element.

Transforms change an element's appearance through translation, rotation, scaling, and skewing, but do not have a time component. You can use the CSS `transform` property to change the location of an element's coordinate space of the CSS visual formatting model, but you need `transitions` or `animation` to make that change occur over time. The `transform` property is covered in *Transforms in CSS* (O'Reilly).

While animation is possible with JavaScript, understanding CSS3 transitions and animations will save you a lot of time and effort if you need to animate anything on the Web. Generally, it will also save your users' CPU and battery compared to JavaScript.

Used correctly, CSS animations and transitions can give your web applications life and depth. While this booklet focuses on *how* to transition and animate elements in your documents, understanding *when* to use animation can improve your user experience (UX) as well. By adding the dimension of time, animating can help your UX communicate on a different level.

## 12 Basic Principles of Animation

Well before the advent of the Web, animators at Disney came up with 12 principles for cartoon animation. Some of these principles are very relevant to CSS animation as well.

According to the "bible of animation"—*The Illusion of Life: Disney Animation* by Frank Thomas and Ollie Johnston—there are 12 basic principles for animation, including:

*Squash and stretch*
Depending on what something is made of, objects deform under motion. *Squashing and stretching* gives the illusion of weight and volume to an object or character as it bounces or otherwise moves. For example, when a ball bounces, it's squashed as it hits the ground and stretches as it heads upward.

*Anticipation*
Users may not understand an animation unless there is a sequence of actions that leads clearly from one activity to the next. They must *anticipate* or expect a change before it actually occurs. In cartoons, it's a movement preparing the viewer for a major action the character is about to perform, like a knee bending before a jump. On the Web, it could be a button depression before the start of the more extensive animation that starts when the button is selected.

Guide your users mentally to where they should focus before initiating the main effect, especially if the start of the animation is important.

*Staging*
In a cartoon, *staging* is the presentation of an idea so it is unmistakably clear. On the Web, staging is directing the user's attention to an action, such as a small jiggle of the call-to-action button. Staging helps guide users through the story or idea being told: for example, through the steps of a check-out process.

*Straight ahead action and pose to pose*
There are two main approaches to animation on the big screen. In the *straight ahead* action approach, the animator starts at the first drawing and works drawing to drawing to the end of a scene. In *pose to pose*, the animator draws the main points within an animation and creates (or has an assistant create) the points in between later. While seemingly only applicable to storyboarding, this principle is also related to drawing keyframes and how the animation fills in the space or time between them.

With CSS animations, when we animate image sprites to create motion, we are emulating the Straight Ahead approach. This is described when we cover the steps values of the `animation-timing-function` property (see "The step timing functions" on page 86). In most animation scenarios, we let the browser be our assistant, defining specific points, or poses, within the animation and allowing the browser to interpolate property values as it animates from pose to pose, or keyframe definition to keyframe definition.

## Follow-through and overlapping action

*Follow-through* is the inclusion of additional motion when the main animation concludes. For example, if a character is running and stops, her hair and clothes were likely bouncing and fall back into place after her legs and body cease moving, catching up to the main mass of the character. Nothing stops all at once.

*Overlapping action* is when some components are slightly delayed after other components change direction, like the way Wile E. Coyote's legs keep moving forward as he drops off a cliff. His ears take a moment to follow.

If your CSS animations ever become complex enough to require follow-through and overlapping action, timing will be critical to making your effects work.

## Slow in and slow out

Just like cars don't start and end at full speed—rather, they accelerate from stopped to full speed and decelerate back to zero—slow ins and slow outs make animation more lifelike and soften the action. Only mechanical animations will proceed at a linear speed.

The *slow in and slow out* principle states that the beginning and end of an animation are more interesting than its middle; and therefore, unless it's mechanical, the animation should proceed fastest in the middle of the animation, with a slower start and slower end. With cartoon animation, the effect is created by having more cells at the ends and fewer in the middle of the action. With CSS, this effect is created by setting cubic Bézier timing functions to something other than `linear` (see "The `transition-timing-function` Property" on page 24).

## Arcs

The *arcs* principle states that almost all actions follow an arc or slightly circular path. Think of your hand moving back and forth as you walk: your hand arcs back and forth rather than always staying at an equal distance from the ground.

Linear animations can be very mechanical. Arcs can be achieved with granular control within a keyframe animation. Because of this, CSS developers often use CSS animations instead of transitions; animations offer more granularity in creating an arced path, while CSS transitions only allow for moving between two states. However, with some cubic Bézier timing functions, creating an arc with CSS transitions is actually not only possible, but fairly simple.

## Secondary action

*Secondary actions* can enrich a main action by adding dimension, supplementing or reinforcing the main action and giving the scene more life. If you include secondary actions, the animations should work together in support of one another.

For example, if your main animation drops a module onto a page, a secondary action might be the main call-to-action button within the module dropping into place, then finishing its action a little after the main module has finished animating in. A secondary action should reinforce the main action. It is OK to literally "think outside the box" and animate a child element differently from its parent.

*Timing*

*Timing* is likely the most important of the principles in this list when it comes to animation. While in traditional animation it's based on the number of frames, in CSS animation it has more to do with creating the appropriate amount of time to read the motion, but not so long as to make the site appear slow. Timing includes not just the duration of the animation (see "The `animation-duration` Property" on page 66), but also the delay ("The `animation-delay` Property" on page 71) and timing function ("The `animation-timing-function` Property" on page 83).

There are no right answers when it comes to timing. Expertise in timing comes with experience and experimentation, if it comes at all. I recommend using trial and error to refine the timing of your animation, then cut your times in half: while you may want your animation to progress slowly enough to grok the difference in times and discover what is the best combination of duration, delay, and progression, you don't want your site to appear slow.

*Exaggeration*

*Exaggeration* is the highlighting of movements beyond their natural state to call attention to what you want the user to focus on. A tiny bit of exaggeration can give added life to an animation and actually make it look more realistic. Use good taste and common sense: exaggeration is not extreme distortion, but rather a slight distortion that gives emphasis without being so exaggerated as to be visibly distorted for your visitors.

*Solid drawing*

The *solid drawing* principle includes the principles of drawing or coding forms that convey the illusion of three dimensions, with weight and solid form. In CSS, this includes using box shadows, gradients, and transforms, giving your content the illusion of being three-dimensional. If you aren't doing 3D animation or spriting, this principle is only tangentially related to web animation, as on the Web, we're drawing with CSS in a two-dimensional space.

*Appeal*

The *appeal* principle has to do with charisma, believability, and interest. Appeal on the Web includes an easy-to-read design, clear drawing, and motion that will capture and involve the visitor's interest. The animation has to appeal to the mind as well as to the eye.

There's a nice video explaining the 12 principles of animation at *https://vimeo.com/93206523*, and a nice display of all of the principles can be found at The Illusion of Life (*http://the12principles.tumblr.com*).

# Animation and Transition Considerations

Flash animation, animated banner ads, and Geocities animated GIFs from 1996 have given animation a bad name. In reality, it isn't that animation itself is bad; it's the way those animations were implemented that led to bad user experiences. With CSS, we can create animations and transitions that improve and augment user experience. Animation can give the appearance of life to two-dimensional, lifeless objects and give understanding to objects that have no meaning. But with great power comes great responsibility.

Animations can be used for good: a small animation can help inform the user that the state of an object has changed, or can occupy the user's attention so they don't notice a slow loading time.

The most important principle is timing and it's the most difficult to fine-tune. Unlike cartoons, timing in CSS means milliseconds, not frames. There is no magic value of milliseconds for the duration. Depending on the timing function, you may want to add a few milliseconds for the effect to feel natural. A developer-defined cubic Bézier timing function that creates a bounce might work better with a bit more time than a simple `ease-in` timing function. Just ensure the animation is short enough for your site to feel responsive rather than slow.

If you have many animations in your site or application, think of timing as a choreography of animations. There is no "right" number of animations. It's not the number of animations, it's the design behind it.

All your animations should feel related. If there is a mix and match of delays, timings, and timing functions, the animations may seem unrelated. Choreograph your animations to ensure a cohesive feel among all the moving parts. Make sure your animations are making your site more sophisticated, more modern, and more trustworthy.

It is up to your designers to design animations that have purpose and style. It's up to this book to teach you how to implement those animations.

# CHAPTER 2

# Transitions

CSS transitions allow us to animate CSS properties from an original value to a new value over time when a property value changes.

Normally, when a CSS property value changes—when a "style change event" occurs—the change is instantaneous. The new property value replaces the old property in the milliseconds it takes to repaint (or reflow and repaint if necessary) the affected content. Most value changes seem instantaneous, taking less than 16 ms[1] to render. Even if the changes takes longer, it is a single step from one value to the next. For example, when changing a background color on hover, the background changes from one color to the next, with no gradual transition. CSS transitions enable us to smoothly animate CSS properties from an original value to a new value over time as the style recomputation proceeds:

```
button {
    color: magenta;
    transition: color 200ms ease-in 50ms;
}

button:hover {
    color: rebeccapurple;
    transition: color 200ms ease-out 50ms;
}
```

---

[1] Changing a background image may take longer than 16 milliseconds to decode and repaint to the page. This isn't a transition; it is just poor performance.

Transitions allow the values of CSS animatable properties to change over time, providing for simple animations.[2] For example, instead of instantaneously changing a button's `color` on hover, with CSS transitions the button can be set to gradually fade from `magenta` to `rebeccapurple` over 200 milliseconds, even adding a 50-millisecond delay before transitioning. Changing a color, no matter how long it takes, is a transition. But by adding the CSS `transition` property, the color change can be gradual.

You can use CSS transitions today, even if you still support IE9 or older browsers. If a browser doesn't support CSS transition properties, the change will be immediate instead of gradual, which is fine and accessible. If the property or property values specified aren't animatable, again, the change will be immediate instead of gradual.

Because transitions are simply progressive enhancements, there is no reason to not use them today.

## CSS Transitions

CSS transitions provide a way to control how a property changes from one value to the next over time. We can make the property value change gradually, creating pleasant and, hopefully, unobtrusive effects.

The CSS transition properties can be used to animate CSS property values smoothly, following an acceleration curve, after an optional delay, from a previous value to a new value over a specified length of time. CSS transitions let you decide which properties to animate, how long to wait before the animation starts, how long the transition should take, and how the transition will proceed. All these features are customizable.

Sometimes you want instantaneous value changes. Though we used link colors as an example in the preceding section, link colors should change instantly on hover, informing sighted users an interaction is occurring and that the hovered content is a link. Similarly, options in an autocomplete listbox shouldn't fade in: you want the options to appear instantly, rather than fade in more slowly than the user types. Instantaneous value changes are often the best user experience.

At other times, you might want to make a property value change more gradually, bringing attention to what is occurring.

---

2  There is a pending resolution in the CSS Working Group stating that nonanimatable properties should obey transitions. This will likely not be web-compatible and will probably be reverted.

For example, you may want to make a card game more realistic by taking 200 milliseconds to animate the flipping of a card ▶[3], as the user may not realize what happened if there is no animation.

As another example, you may want your site's drop-down menus to expand or become visible over 200 milliseconds (instead of instantly) which may be jarring. With CSS transitions, you can make a drop-down menu appear slowly. In Figure 2-1, we are transitioning the submenu's height and opacity over 200 milliseconds. ▶ The menu changes from hidden to fully opaque and expanded. This is a common use for CSS transitions, which we will also explore later in this chapter.

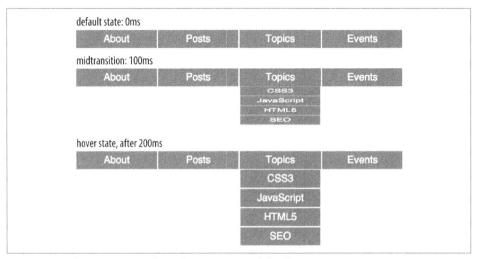

*Figure 2-1. Transition initial, midtransition, and final state*

In this chapter, we cover the four transition properties and the transition shorthand that not only make our transition possible but very easy to implement.

# Fallbacks: Transitions Are Enhancements

Transitions have excellent browser support. All browsers, including Safari, Chrome, Opera, Firefox, Edge, and Internet Explorer (starting with IE10) support CSS transitions.

Transitions are user-interface (UI) enhancements. Lack of full support should not prevent you from including them. If a browser doesn't support CSS transitions, the changes you are attempting to transition will still be applied: they will just "transi-

---

3 All of the examples in this chapter can be found at *http://standardista.com/transitions*.

tion" from the initial state to the end state instantaneously when the style recomputation occurs.

Your users may miss out on an interesting (or possibly annoying) effect, but will not miss out on any content.

As transitions are generally progressive enhancements, there is no need to polyfill for archaic IE browsers. While you could use a JavaScript polyfill for IE9 and earlier, and prefix your transitions for Android 4.3 and earlier, there is likely little need to do so.

# Transition Properties

In CSS, transitions are written using four transition properties: `transition-property`, `transition-duration`, `transition-timing-function`, and `transition-delay`, along with the `transition` property as a shorthand for the four longhand properties.

To create the drop-down navigation from Figure 2-1, we used all four CSS transition properties:

```
nav li ul {
    transition-property: transform;
    transition-duration: 200ms;
    transition-timing-function: ease-in;
    transition-delay: 50ms;
    transform: scale(1, 0);
    transform-origin: top center;
}
nav li:hover ul {
    transform: scale(1, 1);
}
```

This example defines the transition for our drop-down navigation example in Figure 2-1. The style change in this scenario is caused by hovering over navigational elements.

 While we are using the `:hover` state for our style change event in our transition examples, you can transition properties in other scenarios too. For example, you might add or remove a class, or otherwise change the state—say, by changing an input from `:invalid` to `:valid` or from `:checked` to `:not(:checked)`. Or you might append a table row at the end of a zebra-striped table or list item at the end of a list with styles based on `:nth-last-of-type` selectors.

In the navigation pictured in Figure 2-1, the initial state of the nested lists is `transform: scale(1, 0)` with a `transform-origin: top center`. The final state is `transform: scale(1, 1)`: the `transform-origin` remains the same.

In this example, the transition properties define a transition on the `transform` property: when the new `transform` value is set on `hover`, the nested unordered list will scale to its original, default size, changing smoothly between the old value of `transform: scale(1, 0)` and the new value of `transform: scale(1, 1)` over a period of 200 milliseconds. This transition will start after a 50-millisecond delay, and will ease in, proceeding slowly at first, then picking up speed as it progresses.

Transitions are declared along with the regular styles on an element. Whenever a target property changes, if a transition is set on that property, the browser will apply a transition to make the change gradual. While the most common initiation of a transition is changing property values from a default state to a hovered state, transitions also work if the property is changed by adding a class, manipulating the DOM, or otherwise changing the state.

You can declare transition properties in the initial state, the changed state, or in both the initial and changed states. If you only declare the transition on the initial state, when the state changes, it will transition to the changed state as you indicate with CSS transition properties. If and when it changes back to the initial state, the transition timing is reversed. You can override this default reverse transition by declaring different transitions in both the initial and changed states.

By *initial state*, I mean a state that matches the element on page load. This could be a state that the element always has, such as properties set on an element selector versus a :hover state for that element, or a content editable element that may get :focus: ▶

```
/* selector that matches element all the time */
p[contenteditable] {
    background-color: rgba(0, 0, 0, 0);
}

/* selector that matches element some of the time */
p[contenteditable]:focus {
    /* overriding declaration */
    background-color: rgba(0, 0, 0, 0.1);
}
```

In this example, the fully transparent declaration is always the initial value, changing when the user gives it focus. This is what I mean when I use *initial* or *default* value throughout this chapter. The transition properties included in the selector that matches the element all the time will impact that element whenever the state changes, whether it is from the initial state to the focused state (as in the preceding example) or any other altered state, such as a hover state; or when properties are changed with the dynamic addition of a class.

An initial state could also be a temporary state that may change, such as a :checked checkbox or a :valid form control, or even a class that gets toggled on and off:

```
/* selector that matches element some of the time */
input:valid {
    border-color: green;
}

/* selector that matches element some of the time,
   when the prior selector does NOT match. */
input:invalid {
    border-color: red;
}

/* selector that matches element some of the time,
   whether the input is valid or invalid */
input:focus {
    /* alternative declaration */
    border-color: yellow;
}
```

In this example, either the :valid or :invalid selector matches, but never both. The :focus selector, as shown in Figure 2-2, matches some of the time, when the input has focus, whether the input is matching the :valid or :invalid selector simultaneously. In this case, when we refer to the initial state, we are referring to the original value, which could be either valid or invalid. In this scenario, the changed state can be the opposite of the initial :valid or :invalid value. The :focus state is another altered state. ⏵

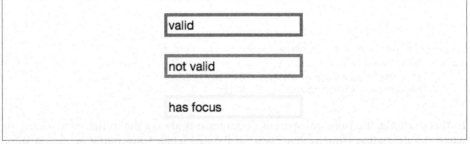

*Figure 2-2. The input's appearance in the valid, invalid, and focused states*

Generally, you want to declare the transition properties at minimum on the selector that applies to the element all the time. In the preceding contenteditable scenario, it is the first rule. The second scenario is not as clear-cut: if the transition is only set on the :invalid state, the color will transition from red to green as the state of the input changes from invalid to valid, and it will transition from red to yellow when an invalid input receives focus. However, it will not slowly transition from green to yellow, or yellow back to green, when a valid input receives or loses focus. Similarly, the border will transition as it changes from or to the invalid state with a red border; if the input is valid, there will be no transition when the user gives or removes focus.

In this second scenario, we could put the transition on the :focus selector, as generally the value will change from valid to invalid or the reverse when the input has focus. Preferably, however, you will want to put the transition on both the possible initial states, or all three states.

In other words, if you always want the property to transition, you likely want to put the transition on *all* the states. The transition properties that are used are the ones in the *destination state*; the new values of the transition properties are used to transition to the new value of the property:

```
nav li ul {
    transition-property: transform;
    transition-duration: 200ms;
    transition-timing-function: ease-in;
    transition-delay: 50ms;
    transform: scale(1, 0);
    transform-origin: top center;
}
nav li:hover ul {
    transition-property: transform;
    transition-duration: 2s;
    transition-timing-function: linear;
    transition-delay: 1s;
    transform: scale(1, 1);
}
```

This provides a horrible user experience, but I've included it to show a point. ⊙ When hovered over, the opening of the navigation takes a full two seconds. When closing, it quickly closes over 0.2 seconds. The transition properties in the destination or hover state are used when hovering over the list item. When no longer hovered over, as it returns to the default scaled-down state, the transition properties of the default properties it is returning to—the nav li ul condition—are used.

In our example, we don't want horrible UX. We will omit the slow transition, and instead allow the browser to reverse the transition on mouse out: ⊙

```
nav li ul {
    transition-property: transform;
    transition-duration: 200ms;
    transition-timing-function: ease-in;
    transition-delay: 50ms;
    transform: scale(1, 0);
    transform-origin: top center;
}
nav li:hover ul {
    transform: scale(1, 1);
}
```

To create a simple CSS hover transition, such as the expansion of nested list items in the preceding navigation example, we declare property values in two states: the default or initial state of the element and the hovered state of the element. The initial or original state of the element is declared in the default style declaration. The changed properties, or final or destination state of the element, are declared within a :hover style block. If no transition is set, the nested unordered list scales to its default height instantly on hover.

To transition this expansion, we add the transition functions using the `transition-*` properties of `transition-property`, `transition-duration`, `transition-timing-function`, and `transition-delay`, or the `transition` shorthand. In our example, we will be adding the transition properties only in the default style declaration. When the transition is declared in the style block of the initial state of the element, the transition will be applied as the element changes from the initial state to the changed or destination state and applied in reverse as it changes back to the initial state from the changed state.

In our example, when the user stops hovering over the parent navigational element or the child drop-down menu, the drop-down menu will wait 50 milliseconds before closing over 200 milliseconds, using `ease-out` as the timing function, reversing the transition declared in the default state. As we saw in our bad UX example, the reverse transition timing function, duration, and delay in the reverting direction can be overridden by providing different transition property values in the default and changed-state style blocks.

While the four transition properties can be declared separately, you will probably always use the shorthand. We'll take a look at the four properties individually first so you have a good understanding of what each one does, and then we'll cover the `transition` shorthand, which is what you will likely use in your code.

Let's look at the four properties in greater detail.

## The `transition-property` Property

The `transition-property` property specifies the names of the CSS properties you want to transition. And, yes, it's weird to say "the `transition-property` property."

---

### transition-property

**Values:**      none|<single-property>#

**Initial value:**  all

---

| **Applies to:** | All elements, :before and :after pseudo-elements |
|---|---|
| **Inherited:** | No |

The value for the `transition-property` is a comma-separated list of properties; the keyword `none` if you want no properties transitioned; or the default `all`, which means "transition all the transitionable properties." You can also include the keyterm `all` within a comma-separated list of properties.

If you include `all` as the only keyterm—or default to `all`—all the transitionable properties will transition in unison.

Let's say you want to change a box's appearance on hover:

```css
div {
    color: #ff0000;
    border: 1px solid #00ff00;
    border-radius: 0;
    transform: scale(1) rotate(0deg);
    opacity: 1;
    box-shadow: 3px 3px rgba(0, 0, 0, 0.1);
    width: 50px;
    padding: 100px;
}
div:hover {
    color: #000000;
    border: 5px dashed #000000;
    border-radius: 50%;
    transform: scale(2) rotate(-10deg);
    opacity: 0.5;
    box-shadow: -3px -3px rgba(255, 0, 0, 0.5);
    width: 100px;
    padding: 20px;
}
```

When the user hovers over the `div`, every property that has a different value in the default state versus the hovered state will change to the hover-state values. We use the `transition-property` property to define which of those properties we want to animate over time (versus instantly). All the properties will change from the default value to the hovered value on `hover`, but only the animatable properties included in the `transition-property` will transition over time. Nonanimatable properties like `border-style` will change from one value to the next instantly. See "Transitionable properties" on page 18.

## all

If you want to define all the properties to transition at the same time, speed, and pace, use `all`. If `all` is the only value or the last value in the comma-separated value for `transition-property`, all the animatable properties will transition in unison.

If we want to transition all the properties, the following statements are almost equivalent:

```
div {
    color: #ff0000;
    border: 1px solid #00ff00;
    border-radius: 0;
    transform: scale(1) rotate(0deg);
    opacity: 1;
    box-shadow: 3px 3px rgba(0, 0, 0, 0.1);
    width: 50px;
    padding: 100px;
    transition-property: color, border, border-radius, transform, opacity,
        box-shadow, width, padding;
    transition-duration: 1s;
}
```

and

```
div {
    color: #ff0000;
    border: 1px solid #00ff00;
    border-radius: 0;
    transform: scale(1) rotate(0deg);
    opacity: 1;
    box-shadow: 3px 3px rgba(0, 0, 0, 0.1);
    width: 50px;
    padding: 100px;
    transition-property: all;
    transition-duration: 1s;
}
```

Both `transition-property` property declarations will transition all the properties listed—but the former will transition only the eight properties that may change, based on property declarations that may be included in other rule blocks. Those eight property values are included in the same rule block, but they don't have to be.

The `all` in the latter example ensures that *all* animatable property values that would change based on any style change event—no matter which CSS rule block includes the changed property value—transitions over one second. The transition applies to all animatable properties of all elements matched by the selector, not just the properties declared in the same style block as the `all`.

Declaring individual properties means only the properties specifically defined in the value of the `transition-property` transition when the value gets changed—whether those property values are inherited, declared in the same rule block, or applied to the element via a different CSS rule block.

In this case, the first version limits the transition to only the eight properties listed, but enables us to provide more control over how each property will transition. Declaring the properties individually lets us provide different speeds, delays, and/or durations to each property's transition if we declared those transition properties separately:

```
<div class="foo">Hello</div>

div {
    color: #ff0000;
    border: 1px solid #0f0;
    border-radius: 0;
    transform: scale(1) rotate(0deg);
    opacity: 1;
    box-shadow: 3px 3px rgba(0, 0, 0, 0.1);
    width: 50px;
    padding: 100px;
}

.foo {
    color: #00ff00;
    transition-property: color, border, border-radius, transform, opacity,
        box-shadow, width, padding;
    transition-duration: 1s;
}
```

The `transition-property` property does not need to be in the same rule block as the properties that make up its value.

If you want to define the transitions for each property separately, write them all out, separating each of the properties with a comma. If you want to animate almost all the properties at the same time, delay, and pace, with a few exceptions, you can use a combination of `all` and the individual properties you want to transition at different times, speeds, or pace. Make sure to use `all` as the first value:

```
div {
    color: #f00;
    border: 1px solid #00ff00;
    border-radius: 0;
    transform:
    scale(1) rotate(0deg);
    opacity: 1;
    box-shadow: 3px 3px rgba(0, 0, 0, 0.1);
    width: 50px;
    padding: 100px;
    transition-property: all, border-radius,
    opacity; transition-duration: 1s, 2s, 3s;
}
```

The all part of the comma-separated value includes all the properties listed in the example, as well as all the inherited CSS properties, and all the properties defined in any other CSS rule block matching or inherited by the element. In the preceding example, all the properties getting new values will transition at the same duration, delay, and timing function, with the exception of border-radius and opacity, which we've explicitly included separately. Because we included them as part of a comma-separated list after the all, we can transition them at the the same time, delay, and timing function as all the other properties, or we can provide different times, delays, and timing functions for these two properties. In this case, we transition all the properties over one second, except for border-radius and opacity, which we transition over two seconds and three seconds, respectively. We cover transition-duration next.

 Make sure to use all as the first value in your comma-separated value list, as the properties declared before the all will be included in the all, overriding any other transition property values you intended to apply to those now overridden properties.

**none**

While transitioning over time doesn't happen by default, if you do include a CSS transition and want to override that transition in a particular scenario, you can set transition-property: none to override the entire transition and ensure no properties are transitioned. The none; keyword can only be used as a unique value of the property—you can't include it as part of a comma-separated list of properties. If you want to override the animation of fewer than all the properties, you will have to list all of the properties you still want to transition. You can't use the transition-property property to exclude properties; rather, you can only use that property to include them. Another trick would be to set the delay and duration of the property to 0s. That way it will appear instantaneously: no CSS transition is being applied to it.

### Transitionable properties

Not all properties are transitionable, and not all values of some normally transitionable properties can be transitioned. There is a finite list of CSS 2.1 properties that are animatable, which is summarized in "Animatable Properties" on page 47. Realize that as CSS is evolving, new properties are being added. While the animatable properties list is not worth memorizing, the general rule is that if there is a logical midpoint between the initial value and the final value of a property, that property and value type is probably animatable.

By "property and value type," I mean that some properties are animatable, but not all values of those properties are animatable. Numeric values tend to be animatable; keyword values that can't be converted to numeric values generally aren't. Keywords that represent computed values, like `red` (which is converted to an RGB value) are animatable. Keyterms that aren't computed values, like `auto` in `top: auto`, are not. CSS functions that take numeric values as parameters generally are animatable. For example, you can transition from `height: 0` to `height: 200px` as both values are numeric. But even though `height` is an animatable property, `height: auto` is *not* an animatable value, as `auto` in this case is not a computed value.

You *can* transition from `color: red` to `color: slategray`, as the browser converts the colors from named colors to hexadecimal values, which are numeric; the browser can determine the midpoint between two numeric values.

If you accidentally included a property that can't be transitioned, fear not. The browser will simply not transition the property that is not animatable. The entire declaration will not fail. The nonanimatable property or nonexistent CSS property is not exactly ignored. The browser passes over unrecognized or nonanimatable properties, keeping their place in the property list order to ensure that the other comma-separated transition properties described next are not applied on the wrong properties.[4]

Transitions can only occur on properties that are not currently being impacted by a CSS animation. If the element is being animated, properties may still transition, as long as they are not properties that are currently controlled by the animation. CSS animations are covered in Chapter 3.

The behavior of transitions seemingly not adhering to the basics of CSS cascades when an animation on the same element and property is running does not affect whether the transition has started or ended. The cascade is actually being adhered to. Transition events will still fire, confirming the transition occurred.

The length of the `transition-property` list determines the number of items in the `transition-duration`, `transition-timing-function`, and `transition-delay` lists. If the number of values in any or all of these three properties does not match the number of values listed in the `transition-property` value, the browser will ignore any excess values, or repeat values when these other properties have fewer values in their comma-separated list than the `transition-property` property. For this reason, the order of the values in the `transition-property` value may be important, just as it is important for other transition properties.

---

4 This might change. The CSS Working Group is considering making all property values animatable, switching from one value to the next at the midpoint of the timing function if there is no midpoint between the pre and post values.

If you include a property that is not animatable (like a border-style value change) or a nonexistent property (such as a property name with a typo in it), the transition-property will still work. Unrecognized words or properties that are not animatable are not ignored. Rather, they are kept in the list of properties to ensure that values from other comma-separated transition properties, such as transition-duration, are applied in the right order.

However, if you have a syntax error, like a missing comma between two property names or a space within a property name, that transition-property property declaration will be ignored. Similarly, if you include the terms none, inherit, or initial, as per the specification, the entire property exists, but fails, so should be ignored. This is not the case in some browsers, however. Safari 8 and IE Edge 12 treat none, inherit, and initial in a list of comma-separated properties as unrecognized or nonanimatable properties.

### Transition event: transitionend

A transitionend event occurs at the end of every transition, in each direction, for every property that is transitioned over any amount of time or after any delay, whether the property is declared individually or is part of the all declaration. For some seemingly single property declarations, there will be several transitionend events, as every animatable property within a shorthand property gets its own transitionend event.

In the preceding example, when the transition concludes, there will be well over eight transitionend events. For example, the border-radius transition alone produces four transitionend events, one each for:

```
border-bottom-left-radius
border-bottom-right-radius
border-top-right-radius
border-top-left-radius
```

The padding property is also a shorthand for four longhand properties:

```
padding-top
padding-right
padding-bottom
padding-left
```

The border shorthand property produces eight transitionend events: four values for border-width and four for border-color, both of which are shorthand declaration themselves:

```
border-left-width
border-right-width
border-top-width
border-bottom-width
```

```
border-top-color
border-left-color
border-right-color
border-bottom-color
```

There are no `transitionend` events for `border-style` properties, as `border-style` is not an animatable property.

How do we know it's not animatable? We can assume it isn't, since there is no logical midpoint between the two values of `solid` and `dashed`. We can confirm by looking up the list of animatable properties (*https://developer.mozilla.org/en-US/docs/Web/CSS/CSS_animated_properties*) or the specifications for the individual properties.

There will be 21 `transitionend` events in our scenario in which 8 specific properties are listed, as those 8 include several shorthand properties that have different values in the pre and post states. In the case of `all`, there will be at least 21 `transitionend` events: one for each of the longhand values making up the 8 properties we know are included in the pre and post states, and possibly from others that are inherited or declared in other style blocks impacting the element: ▶

```
document.querySelector('div').addEventListener('transitionend',
    function (e) {
        console.log(e.propertyName);
});
```

The `transitionend` event includes three event specific attributes: 1) `propertyName`, which is the name of the CSS property that just finished transitioning; 2) `pseudoElement`, which is the pseudoelement upon which the transition occurred, preceded by two semicolons, or an empty string if the transition was on a regular DOM node; and 3) `elapsedTime`, which is the amount of time the transition took to run, in seconds, which is generally the time listed in the `transition-duration` property.

The `transitionend` event only occurs if the property successfully transitions to the new value. The `transitioned` event doesn't fire if the transition was interrupted by another change to the same property on the same element.

When the properties return to their initial value, another `transitionend` event occurs. This event occurs as long as the transition started, even if it didn't finish transitioning in the original direction.

# The `transition-duration` Property

The `transition-duration` property takes as its value a comma-separated list of lengths of time, in seconds (`s`) or milliseconds (`ms`), it should take to transition from the original property values to the final property values.

## transition-duration

| | |
|---|---|
| **Values:** | `<time>#` |
| **Initial value:** | `0s` |
| **Applies to:** | All elements, `:before` and `:after` pseudo-elements |
| **Inherited:** | No |

The `transition-duration` property dictates how long it should take for each property to transition from the original value to the new value. If reverting between two states, and the duration is only declared in one of those states, the transition will take the amount of time declared to revert to the previous state:

```
input:invalid {
    transition-duration: 1s;
    background-color: red;
}

input:valid {
    transition-duration: 0.2s;
    background-color: green;
}
```

If different values for the `transition-duration` are declared, the duration of the transition will be the `transition-duration` value declared in the rule block it is transitioning to. In the preceding example, it will take 1 second for the input to change to a red background when it becomes invalid, and only 200 milliseconds to transition to a green background when it becomes valid. ▶

The value of the `transition-duration` property should be declared as a positive value in either seconds (`s`) or milliseconds (`ms`). The time unit of `ms` or `s` is required by the specification, even if the duration is set to `0s`. By default, properties simply change from one value to the next instantly. In line with this, the default value for the duration of a transition is `0s`, meaning the transition is immediate, showing no animation.

Unless there is a positive value for `transition-delay` set on a property, if `transition-duration` is omitted, it is as if no `transition-property` declaration had been applied—with no `transitionend` event occuring. As long as the total time set for a transition to occur is greater than 0s—which can happen with a duration of 0s or when the `transition-duration` is omitted and defaults to `0s`, if there is a positive `transition-delay` value—the transition will still be applied and a `transitionend` event will occur if the transition finishes.

Negative values for `transition-duration` are invalid, and, if included, will invalidate the entire property value.

Using the same super-long `transition-property` declaration, we can declare a single duration for all the properties or individual durations for each property, or we can make alternate properties animate for the same length of time. We can declare a single duration that applies to all properties during the transition by including a single `transition-duration` value:

```
div {
    color: #ff0000;
    ...
    transition-property: color, border, border-radius, transform, opacity,
        box-shadow, width, padding;
    transition-duration: 200ms;
}
```

We could have instead declared the same number of comma-separated time values for the `transition-duration` property value as the CSS properties we enumerated in the `transition-property` property value. If we want each property to transition over a different length of time, we have to include a different comma-separated value for each property name declared:

```
div {
    color: #ff0000;
    ...
    transition-property: color, border, border-radius, transform, opacity,
        box-shadow, width, padding;
    transition-duration: 200ms, 180ms, 160ms, 140ms, 120ms, 100ms, 1s, 2s;
}
```

If the number of properties declared does not match the number of durations declared, the browser has specific rules on how to handle the mismatch. If there are more durations than properties, the extra durations are ignored. If there are more properties than durations, the durations are repeated. In this example, `color`, `border-radius`, `opacity`, and `width` have a duration of 100 ms; `border`, `transform`, `box-shadow`, and `padding` will be set to 200 ms:

```
div {
    ...
    transition-property: color, border, border-radius, transform, opacity,
        box-shadow, width, padding;
    transition-duration: 100ms, 200ms;
}
```

If we declare exactly two comma-separated durations, every odd property will transition over the first time declared, and every even property will transition over the second time value declared.

If a transition is too slow, the website will appear slow or unresponsive, drawing unwanted focus to what should be a subtle effect. If a transition is too fast, it may be too subtle to be noticed. While you can declare any positive length of time you want for your transitions, your goal is likely to provide an enhanced rather than annoying user experience. Effects should last long enough to be seen, but not so long as to be noticeable. Generally, the best effects range between 100 and 200 milliseconds, creating a visible, yet not distracting, transition.

We want a good user experience for our drop-down menu, so we set both properties to transition over 200 milliseconds:

```
nav li ul {
    transition-property: transform, opacity;
    transition-duration: 200ms;
    ...
}
```

## The `transition-timing-function` Property

Do you want your transition to start off slow and get faster, start off fast and end slower, advance at an even keel, jump through various steps, or even bounce? The `transition-timing-function` provides a way to control the pace of the transition. The `transition-timing-function` property describes how the transition proceeds as it is being executed.

<table>
<tr><td colspan="2" align="center"><code>transition-timing-function</code></td></tr>
<tr><td>Values:</td><td><code>&lt;timing-function&gt;#</code></td></tr>
<tr><td>Initial value:</td><td><code>ease</code></td></tr>
<tr><td>Applies to:</td><td>All elements, <code>:before</code> and <code>:after</code> pseudo-elements</td></tr>
<tr><td>Inherited:</td><td>No</td></tr>
</table>

The `transition-timing-function` values include `ease`, `linear`, `ease-in`, `ease-out`, `ease-in-out`, `step-start`, `step-end`, `steps(n, start)`—where n is the number of steps—`steps(n, end)`, and `cubic-bezier(x1, y1, x2, y2)`. These values are also the valid values for the `animation-timing-function` and are described in great detail in Chapter 3.

The non-step keyword are easing timing functions employing cubic Bézier mathematical functions to provide smooth curves. The specification provides for five predefined easing functions, but you can describe your own precise timing function by defining your own `cubic-bezier()` function, as shown in Table 2-1.

*Table 2-1. Supported keyterms for cubic Bézier timing functions*

| Timing function | Definition | cubic-bezier value |
| --- | --- | --- |
| `ease` | Starts slow, then speeds up, then ends very slowly | `cubic-bezier(0.25, 0.1, 0.25, 1)` |
| `linear` | Proceeds at the same speed throughout transition | `cubic-bezier(0, 0, 1, 1)` |
| `ease-in` | Starts slow, then speeds up | `cubic-bezier(0.42, 0, 1, 1)` |
| `ease-out` | Starts fast, then slows down | `cubic-bezier(0, 0, 0.58, 1)` |
| `ease-in-out` | Similar to ease; faster in the middle, with a slow start but not as slow at the end | `cubic-bezier(0.42, 0, 0.58, 1)` |
| `cubic-bezier()` | Specifies a cubic-bezier curve | `cubic-bezier(x1, y1, x2, y2)` |

Cubic Bézier curves, including the underlying curves defining the five named easing functions defined in Table 2-1 and displayed in Figure 2-3, take four numeric parameters. For example, `linear` is the same as `cubic-bezier(0, 0, 1, 1)`. The first and third cubic Bézier function parameter values need to be between 0 and +1.

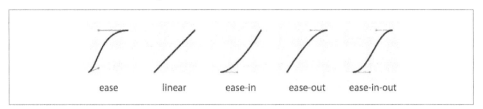

*Figure 2-3. Supported cubic Bézier named functions incude* `ease`, `linear`, `ease-in`, `ease-out`, *and* `ease-in-out`

If you've taken six years of calculus, the method of writing a cubic Bézier function might make sense; otherwise, it's likely you'll want to stick to one of the five basic timing functions. There are online tools that let you play with different values, such as cubic-bezier.com, which lets you compare the common keywords against each other, or against your own cubic Bézier function.

The predefined key terms are fairly limited. To better follow the principles of animation (refer back to "12 Basic Principles of Animation" on page 1), you may want to use a cubic Bézier function with four float values instead of the predefined key words.

As shown in Figure 2-4, the website easings.net provides many additional cubic Bézier function values you can use to provide for a more realistic, delightful animation.

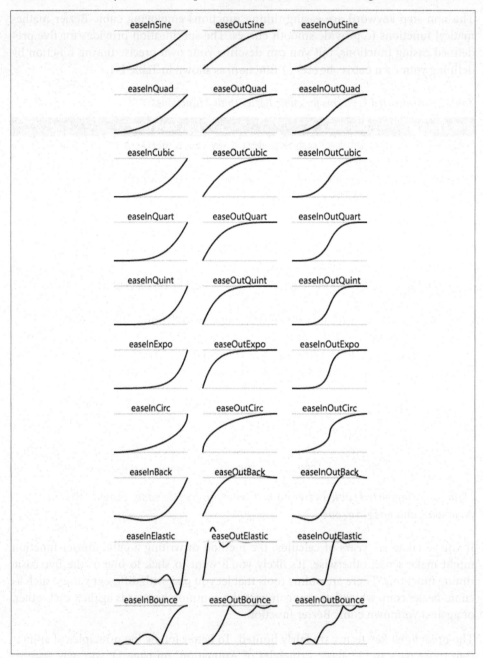

Figure 2-4. Useful author-defined cubic Bézier functions

While the authors of the site named their animations, the preceding names are not part of the CSS specifications, and must be written as follows:

| Unofficial name | Cubic Bézier function value |
| --- | --- |
| easeInSine | cubic-bezier(0.47, 0, 0.745, 0.715) |
| easeOutSine | cubic-bezier(0.39, 0.575, 0.565, 1) |
| easeInOutSine | cubic-bezier(0.445, 0.05, 0.55, 0.95) |
| easeInQuad | cubic-bezier(0.55, 0.085, 0.68, 0.53) |
| easeOutQuad | cubic-bezier(0.25, 0.46, 0.45, 0.94) |
| easeInOutQuad | cubic-bezier(0.455, 0.03, 0.515, 0.955) |
| easeInCubic | cubic-bezier(0.55, 0.055, 0.675, 0.19) |
| easeOutCubic | cubic-bezier(0.215, 0.61, 0.355, 1) |
| easeInOutCubic | cubic-bezier(0.645, 0.045, 0.355, 1) |
| easeInQuart | cubic-bezier(0.895, 0.03, 0.685, 0.22) |
| easeOutQuart | cubic-bezier(0.165, 0.84, 0.44, 1) |
| easeInOutQuart | cubic-bezier(0.77, 0, 0.175, 1) |
| easeInQuint | cubic-bezier(0.755, 0.05, 0.855, 0.06) |
| easeOutQuint | cubic-bezier(0.23, 1, 0.32, 1) |
| easeInOutQuint | cubic-bezier(0.86, 0, 0.07, 1) |
| easeInExpo | cubic-bezier(0.95, 0.05, 0.795, 0.035) |
| easeOutExpo | cubic-bezier(0.19, 1, 0.22, 1) |
| easeInOutExpo | cubic-bezier(1, 0, 0, 1) |
| easeInCirc | cubic-bezier(0.6, 0.04, 0.98, 0.335) |
| easeOutCirc | cubic-bezier(0.075, 0.82, 0.165, 1) |
| easeInOutCirc | cubic-bezier(0.785, 0.135, 0.15, 0.86) |

| Unofficial name | Cubic Bézier function value |
|---|---|
| easeInBack | cubic-bezier(0.6, -0.28, 0.735, 0.045) |
| easeOutBack | cubic-bezier(0.175, 0.885, 0.32, 1.275) |
| easeInOutBack | cubic-bezier(0.68, -0.55, 0.265, 1.55) |

There are also step timing functions available, with two predefined step values:

| Timing function | Definition |
|---|---|
| step-start | Stays on the final keyframe throughout transition. Equal to steps(1, start). |
| step-end | Stays on the initial keyframe throughout transition. Equal to steps(1, end). |
| steps(n, start) | Displays *n* stillshots, where the first stillshot is n/100 percent of the way through the transition. |
| steps(n, end) | Displays *n* stillshots, staying on the initial values for the first n/100 percent of the time. |

As Figure 2-5 shows, the stepping functions show the progression of the transition from the initial value to the final value in steps, rather than as a smooth curve.

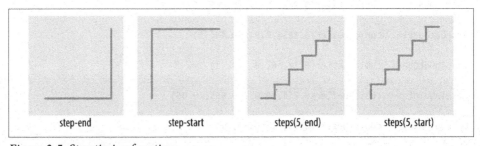

Figure 2-5. Step timing functions

The step functions allow you to divide the transition over equidistant steps. The functions define the number and direction of steps. There are two direction options: start and end. With start, the first step happens at the animation start. With end, the last step happens at the animation end. For example, steps(5, end) would jump through the equidistant steps at 0%, 20%, 40%, 60%, and 80%; and steps(5, start) would jump through the equidistant steps at 20%, 40%, 60%, 80%, and 100%.

The step-start function is the same as steps(1, start). When you use it, the property value stays on the final value from the beginning until the end of the transition. The step-end function, which is the same as steps(1, end), sits on the initial value of the property, staying there through the transition's duration.

Continuing on with the same super-long `transition-property` declaration, we can declare a single timing function for all the properties or individual timing functions for each property, or we can make every even property have one timing function, while every odd property proceeds at a separate pace:

```
div {
    ...
    transition-property: color, border-width, border-color, border-radius,
        transform, opacity, box-shadow, width, padding;
    transition-duration: 200ms;
    transition-timing-function: ease-in;
}
```

In the preceding example, we made all the properties transition at the same tempo by including a single time as the `timing-function` value:

```
div {
    ...
    transition-property: color, border-width, border-color, border-radius,
        transform, opacity, box-shadow, width, padding;
    transition-duration: 200ms, 180ms, 160ms, 140ms, 120ms, 100ms, 1s, 2s, 3s;
    transition-timing-function: ease, ease-in, ease-out, ease-in-out, linear,
        step-end, step-start, steps(5, start), steps(3, end);
}
```

We can also create a horrible user experience by making every property transition at a different rhythm. The `transition-timing-function` does not change the time it takes to transition properties: that is set with the `transition-duration` property; but it does change how the transition progresses during that set time:

```
div {
    ...
    transition-property: color, border-width, border-color, border-radius,
        transform, opacity, box-shadow, width, padding;
    transition-duration: 200ms;
    transition-timing-function: ease, ease-in, ease-out, ease-in-out, linear,
        step-end, step-start, steps(5, start), steps(3, end);
}
```

If we include these nine different timing functions for the nine different properties, as long as they have the same transition duration and delay, all the properties start and finish transitioning at the same time. The timing function controls how the transition progresses, but does not alter the time it takes for the transition to finish.

These timing functions are described in great detail in "animation-timing-function" on page 83. The best way to familiarize yourself with the timing functions is to play with them and see which one works best for the effect you're looking for. While testing, set a relatively long `transition-duration` to better visualize the difference[5] between the various functions. At higher speeds, you may not be able to tell the difference with the easing function; just don't forget to set it back to under 200 milliseconds before launching your website:

```
nav li ul {
    transition-property: transform, opacity;
    transition-duration: 200ms;
    transition-timing-function: ease-in;
    ...
}
```

Our navigation example has transitions occurring in two directions: one transition occurs when changing from the default or initial value to the final hovered value. The second transition occurs when the user mouses off the list item and the nested unordered list returns to its previous or initial state. When the user hovers over the dropdown navigation, it transitions open; it transitions closed when the user mouses off.

We want our menu to open and become opaque fairly quickly, while appearing gradual. The `ease-in` value is the best for this. The timing function is reversed in the reverse direction; by default, when returning to the initial values, the transition will run in reverse order, inverting the timing function. It therefore eases in as it opens and eases out as it closes. In this example, `ease-in` was used, so the return trip will appear as if it was set to `ease-out` as it proceeds in the opposite direction, going from open to closed. This is the default behavior, but it can be controlled. Controlling the reverse transition direction is discussed in "In Reverse: Transitioning Back to Baseline" on page 40.

## The `transition-delay` Property

The `transition-delay` property enables you to introduce a time delay between when the change that initiates the transition is applied to an element and when the transition begins.

If you hover over an element that has a color change on `hover` without a transition, the color will change immediately. Similarly, a `transition-delay` of `0s` (the default) means the transition will begin immediately—it will start executing as soon as the state of the element is altered. Otherwise, the time value of the `transition-delay` defines the time offset from the moment the property values would have changed (had no `transition` or `transition-property` been applied) until the property values

---

5  You can test the various `transition-timing-function` examples at *http://www.standardista.com/css3/transitions*.

declared in the `transition` or `transition-property` value begins animating to the next value.

---

# transition-delay

| | |
|---|---|
| **Values:** | `<time>#` |
| **Initial value:** | `0s` |
| **Applies to:** | All elements, `:before` and `:after` pseudo-elements |
| **Inherited:** | No |

---

Including a `transition-delay` with a positive number of milliseconds (`ms`) or seconds (`s`) to delay the transition will delay the onset of the transition effect. The time unit, as `s` or `ms`, is required. Negative values of time are valid. The effects you can create with negative `transition-delays` are described in "Negative values" on page 33.

 Unlike `transition-duration`, negative time values are allowed for the `transition-delay` property.

Continuing with the 8- (or 21-) property `transition-property` declaration, we can make all the properties start transitioning right away by omitting the `transition-delay` property or including it with a value of `0s`—but that's not a very interesting example. For the sake of examples, we could delay the start of all the even-numbered properties, while all the odd-numbered properties start right away, by including two comma-separated values, starting with `0s` or `0ms`:

```
div {
    ...
    transition-property: color, border, border-radius, transform, opacity,
        box-shadow, width, padding;
    transition-duration: 200ms;
    transition-timing-function: linear;
    transition-delay: 0s, 200ms;
}
```

By including `transition-delay: 0s, 200ms` on a series of properties, each taking 200 milliseconds to transition, we make every odd-numbered property begin its transition immediately; all the even-numbered transitions begin their transitions as soon as the odd transitions have completed.

As with `transition-duration` and `transition-timing-function`, when the number of comma-separated `transition-delay` values outnumbers the number of comma-separated `transition-property` values, the extra delay values are ignored. When the number of comma-separated `transition-property` values outnumbers the number of comma-separated `transition-delay` values, the delay values are repeated. In this case, with only two values, the first value (`0s`) is applied to each odd property, providing no delay, and the second value is applied to every even property, providing a 200-millisecond delay. Because we declared the `transition-duration` as `200ms` in this scenario, every evenly numbered property will begin transitioning after 200 milliseconds, which is after every oddly numbered property has finished transitioning:

```
div {
    ...
    transition-property: color, border-width, border-color, border-radius,
        transform, opacity, box-shadow, width, padding;
    transition-duration: 200ms;
    transition-timing-function: linear;
    transition-delay: 0s, 0.2s, 0.4s, 0.6s, 0.8s, 1s, 1.2s, 1.4s, 1.6s;
}
```

We can even declare nine different `transition-delay` values so that each property begins transitioning after the previous property has transitioned. In this example, we declared each transition to last 200 milliseconds with the `transition-duration` property. We then declare a `transition-delay` that provides comma-separated delay values for each property that increment by 200 milliseconds, or 0.2 seconds—the same time as the duration of each property's transition. That means we can make each property start transitioning as soon as the previous property has finished.

We can use math to give every transitioning property different durations and delays, ensuring they all complete transitioning at the same time:

```
div {
    ...
    transition-property: color, border-width, border-color, border-radius,
        transform, opacity, box-shadow, width, padding;
    transition-duration: 1.8s, 1.6s, 1.4s, 1.2s, 1s, 0.8s, 0.6s, 0.4s, 0.2s;
    transition-timing-function: linear;
    transition-delay: 0s, 0.2s, 0.4s, 0.6s, 0.8s, 1s, 1.2s, 1.4s, 1.6s;
}
```

In this example, each property completes transitioning at the 1.8-second mark, but each with a different duration and delay. For each property, the transition-duration value plus the transition-delay value will add up to 1.8 seconds:

```
div {
    ...
    transition-property: color, border-width, border-color, border-radius,
        transform, opacity, box-shadow, width, padding;
    transition-duration: 200ms;
    transition-timing-function: linear;
    transition-delay: 50ms;
}
```

Generally, you want all the transitions to begin at the same time. You can make that happen by including a single transition-delay value, which gets applied to all the properties. In our drop-down menu in Figure 2-1, we include a delay of 50 milliseconds. This delay is not long enough for the user to notice and will not cause the application to appear slow. Rather, a 50-millisecond delay can help prevent the navigation from shooting open unintentionally as the user accidentally passes over, or hovers over, the menu items while moving the cursor from one part of the page or app to another.

### Negative values

A negative time value for transition-delay will make the transition begin immediately, partially through the transition. A negative transition-delay that is smaller than the transition-duration will cause the transition to start immediately, partway through the transition: ▶

```
div {
    transform: translateX(0);
    transition-property: transform;
    transition-duration: 200ms;
    transition-delay: -150ms;
    transition-timing-function: linear;
}
div:hover {
    transform: translateX(200px);
}
```

For example, if you have a transition-delay of -150ms on a 200ms transition, the transition will start three-quarters of the way through the transition and will last 50 milliseconds. In that scenario, with a linear timing function, it will jump to being translated 150px along the x-axis immediately on hover and then animate the translation from 150 pixels to 200 pixels over 50 milliseconds.

If the absolute value of the negative `transition-delay` is greater than or equal to the `transition-duration`, the change of property values is immediate, as if no `transi tion` had been applied, and no `transitionend` event occurs.

When transitioning back from the hovered state to the original state, by default, the same value for the `transition-delay` is applied. In the preceding scenario, with the `transition-delay` not being overridden in the hover state, it will jump 75% of the way back (or 25% of the way through the original transition) and then transition back to the initial state. On mouseout, it will jump to being translated 50 pixels along the x-axis and then take 50 milliseconds to return to its initial position of being translated 0 pixels along the x-axis.

### Improving user experience

If you hover over the navigation item from Figure 2-1, you would expect the drop-down menu to appear immediately. But that isn't the user experience we want. The user may unintentionally hover over the navigation while mousing from one section of the document to another. Waiting for the user to hover over the navigation element for 50 milliseconds before opening the drop-down menu isn't enough of a delay to make the site appear slow but is enough of a delay to ensure menus don't seem to be unintentionally flying open:

```
nav li ul {
    transition-property: transform, opacity;
    transition-duration: 200ms;
    transition-timing-function: ease-in;
    transition-delay: 50ms;
    transform: scale(1, 0);
    transform-origin: top center;
    opacity: 0;
}
nav li:hover ul {
    transform: scale(1, 1);
    opacity: 1;
}
```

In our navigation example, we add a 50-millisecond transition delay. This way, our drop-down menu won't transition immediately if the user accidentally mouses over a link on the way from one part of the document to another. By adding `transition-delay: 50ms`, we can be more confident the user is intentionally hovering over the parent navigation item before opening the drop-down menu.

The browser will also wait 50 milliseconds after the user mouses off the navigational element before transitioning back to the pretransitioned state. When the `transition-delay` is specified somewhere that applies to the element all the time, the `transition-delay` occurs in both transition directions; that means the browser will wait 50 milliseconds after the parent li or its descendant loses hover before closing the drop-down menu.

This 50-millisecond delay before closing occurs whether or not the menu is completely open or even if the user mouses out of the menu before the menu finishes transitioning open. The browser will wait 50 milliseconds before opening the drop-down menu and will also wait 50 milliseconds before closing it—whether or not it was ever fully visible—as long as it had started to open.

This may seem odd, but it improves user experience. Often users accidentally mouse out of a navigational element as they mouse toward an item in the newly opened sub-menu. This 50-millisecond delay in the reverse direction gives the user a 50-millisecond window to get back onto the drop-down menu before it closes. This isn't enough time to completely hover off and back on, but if there are submenus, an accidental mousing over nonnavigation space as the user moves the pointer to a subnavigation may be short enough to not close the navigation completely. If the user doesn't hover over the open menu of the parent tab, the menu will transition back to a closed state. This is a good user experience.

If a mouse user leaves the area after the 50-millisecond delay but before the 200-millisecond duration, the menu will not open fully. Rather, there will be a 50-millisecond delay, and then the menu will revert to its fully closed state. Some browsers will take the full 200 milliseconds to revert; others will spend the same amount of time in the reverse direction as they did in the normal direction. A *reversing shortening factor*, which shortens the reverse transition time of incomplete transitions, is defined in the CSS Transitions specifications and is beginning to be implemented in browsers.

### Reverse direction

When a transitioned property reverts from the final state to the initial state and transition properties are only set on the start or initial state, the delay is repeated and the timing is reversed. If the transition is interrupted and doesn't complete, the duration and delay are not ignored as the properties revert.

When a transition is interrupted before it is able to finish (such as mousing off of our drop-down menu example before it finishes opening), property values are reset to the values they had before the transition began, and the properties will transition back to those values. Because repeating the duration and timing functions on a reverting partial transition can lead to an odd or even bad user experience, the CSS transitions specification provides for making the reverting transition shorter.

In our menu example, we have a `transition-delay` of 50ms set on the default state and no transition properties declared on the hover state; thus, browsers will wait 50 milliseconds before beginning the reverse or closing transition.

When the forward animation finishes transitioning to the final values and the `transitionend` event is fired, all browsers will duplicate the `transition-delay` in the reverse states.

As Table 2-2 shows, if the transition didn't finish—say, if the user moved off the navigation before the transition finished—all browsers except Microsoft Edge will repeat the delay in the reverse direction. Some browsers replicate the `transition-duration` as well, but Edge and Firefox have implemented the specification's reversing shortening factor.

*Table 2-2. Unfinished transition reverse behavior by browser*

| Browser | Reverse delay | Transition time | Elapsed time |
|---------|---------------|-----------------|--------------|
| Chrome 37 | Yes | 200 ms | 0.200s |
| Chrome 42 | Yes | 200 ms | 0.250s |
| Safari 8 | Yes | 200 ms | 0.200s |
| Firefox 41 | Yes | 38 ms | 0.038s |
| Opera 32 | Yes | 200 ms | 0.250s |
| Edge 12 | No | 38 ms | 0.038s |

Let's say the user moves off that menu 75 milliseconds after it started transitioning. This means the drop-down menu will animate closed without ever being fully opened and fully opaque. The browser should have a 50-millisecond delay before closing the menu, just like it waited 50 milliseconds before starting to open it. This is actually a good user experience, as it provides a few milliseconds of delay before closing, preventing jerky behavior if the user accidentally navigates off the menu. As shown in Table 2-2, all browsers do this, except Microsoft Edge. In cases where the original transition has completed, all browsers, including Edge, will repeat the 50-millisecond delay before reverting the transition and closing the menu—but if the original transition did not have time to conclude, Microsoft Edge currently does not wait before reversing the transition. This is true for positive `transition-delay` values.

Even though we only gave the browser 75 milliseconds to partially open the drop-down menu before closing the menu, some browsers will take 200 milliseconds—the full value of the `transition-duration` property—to revert. Other browsers, including Firefox and Edge, have implemented the CSS specification's reversing shortening factor and the reversing-adjusted start value. When implemented, the time to complete the partial transition in the reverse direction will be similar to the original value, though not necessarily exact. For step timing functions, it will be the time it took to complete the last completed step. For `linear` timing functions, the partial durations will be the same in both directions. In the case of our `ease-in` 75-millisecond partial transition duration, the reverse duration is 38.4 milliseconds:

```
div {
    width: 100px;
    transition: width 10s steps(10, start);
}
div:hover {
    width: 200px;
}
```

In the case of a steps timing function, Firefox and Edge will take the time, rounded down to the number of steps the function has completed. For example, if the transition was 10 seconds with 10 steps, and the properties reverted after 3.25 seconds, ending a quarter of the way between the third and fourth steps (completing 3 steps, or 30% of the transition) it will take 3 seconds to revert to the previous values. In the preceding example, the width of our `div` will grow to 130 pixels wide before it begins reverting back to 100 pixels wide on mouseout.

While the reverse duration will be rounded down to the time it took to the last step, the reverse *direction* will be split into the originally declared number of steps, not the number of steps that completed. In our 3.25-second case, it will take 3 seconds to revert through 10 steps. These reverse transition steps will be shorter in duration at 300 milliseconds each, each step shrinking the width by 3 pixels, instead of 10 pixels.

If we were animating a sprite by transitioning the background-position ⊙, this would look really bad. The specification and implementation may change to make the reverse direction take the same number of steps as the partial transition. Other browsers currently take 10 seconds, reverting the progression of the 3 steps over 10 seconds across 10 steps—taking a full second to grow the width in 3-pixel steps.

Browsers that haven't implemented shortened reversed timing, including Chrome, Safari, and Opera, will take the full 10 seconds, instead of only 3, splitting the transition into 10 steps, to reverse the 30% change. Whether the initial transition completed or not, these browsers will take the full value of the initial transition duration, less the absolute value of any negative `transition-delay`, to reverse the transition, no matter the timing function. In the steps case just shown, the reverse direction will take 10 seconds. In our navigation example, it will reverse over 200 milliseconds, whether the navigation has fully scaled up or not.

For browsers that have implemented the reversing timing adjustments, if the timing function is linear, the duration will be the same in both directions. If the timing function is a step function, the reverse duration will be equal to the time it took to complete the last completed step. All other `cubic-bezier` functions will have a duration that is proportional to progress the initial transition made before being interrupted (*https://drafts.csswg.org/css-transitions/transition-reversing-demo*). Negative transition-delay values are also proportionally shortened. Positive delays remain unchanged in both directions.

No browser will have a transitionend for the hover state, as the transition did not end; but all browsers will have a transitionend event in the reverse state when the menu finishes collapsing. The elapsedTime for that reverse transition depends on whether the browser took the full 200 milliseconds to close the menu, or if the browser takes as long to close the menu as it did to partially open the menu. Chrome and Opera include the delay in their elapsedTime value. As of early 2016, this is a bug, and should be fixed soon. All other browsers include only the time the browser spent transitioning back—75 milliseconds for Firefox and Edge, 200 milliseconds for Safari and older versions of Chrome and Android.

To override these values, include transition properties in both CSS rule blocks. While this does not impact the reverse shortening, it does provide more control.

We'll first cover the transition shorthand property, then we'll use that property to set different transitions in the reverse direction.

## The transition Shorthand Property

The transition shorthand property combines the four properties just described—transition-property, transition-duration, transition-timing-function, and transition-delay—into a single property.

---

### transition

| | |
|---|---|
| **Values:** | <single-transition># |
| **Initial value:** | all 0s ease 0s |
| **Applies to:** | All elements, :before and :after pseudo-elements |
| **Inherited:** | No |

---

The transition property accepts the value of none or any number of comma-separated list of *single transitions*. A single transition contains a single property to transition, or the keyword all to transition all the properties—preferably the duration for the transition, and optionally, the timing function and delay.

If a single transition within the transition shorthand omits the property to transition (or the keyword all), the single transition will default to all. If the transition-timing-function value is omitted, it will default to ease. If only one time value is included, that will be the duration, and there will be no delay, as if transition-delay were set to 0s. If two time values are included, the first is the transition-duration and the second is the transition-delay.

Within each single transition, the order of the duration versus the delay is important: the first value that can be parsed as a time will be set as a duration. If an additional time value is found before the comma or the end of the statement, that will be set as the delay:

```
nav li ul {
    transition: transform 200ms ease-in 50ms,
                opacity 200ms ease-in 50ms;
    ...
}

nav li ul {
    transition: all 200ms ease-in 50ms;
      ...
}

nav li ul {
    transition: 200ms ease-in 50ms;
    ...
}
```

The shorthand for our drop-down menu can be written three different ways. In the first example, we included shorthand for each of the two properties. Because we are transitioning all the properties that change on hover, we could use the keyword all, as shown in the second example. And, as all is the default value, we could write the shorthand with just the duration, timing-function and delay. Had we used ease instead of ease-in, we could have omitted the timing function, since ease is the default.

We had to include the duration, or no transition would be visible. In other words, the only portion of the transition property that can be considered required is transition-duration.

If we simply wanted to delay the change from closed menu to open menu without a gradual transition, we would still need to include a duration of 0s. Remember, the first value parsable as time will be set as the duration, and the second one will be set as the delay:

```
nav li ul {
    transition: 0s 200ms; ...
```

This navigation will wait 200 milliseconds, then show the drop-down fully open and opaque with no gradual transition. This is horrible user experience. Though if you switch the selector from nav li ul to *, it might make for an April Fools' joke.

If there is a comma-separated list of transitions (versus just a single declaration) and the word none is included, the entire transition declaration is invalid and will be ignored:

```
div {
    ...
    transition-property: color, border-width, border-color, border-radius,
        transform, opacity, box-shadow, width, padding;
    transition-duration: 200ms, 180ms, 160ms, 140ms, 120ms, 100ms, 1s, 2s, 3s;
    transition-timing-function: ease, ease-in, ease-out, ease-in-out, linear,
        step-end, step-start, steps(5, start), steps(3, end);
    transition-delay: 0s, 0.2s, 0.4s, 0.6s, 0.8s, 1s, 1.2s, 1.4s, 1.6s;
}

div {
    ...
    transition:
        color 200ms,
        border-width 180ms ease-in 200ms,
        border-color 160ms ease-out 400ms,
        border-radius 140ms ease-in-out 600ms,
        transform 120ms linear 800ms,
        opacity 100ms step-end 1s,
        box-shadow 1s step-start 1.2s,
        width 2s steps(5, start) 1.4s,
        padding 3s steps(3, end) 1.6s;
}
```

The two preceding CSS rule blocks are functionally equivalent: you can declare comma-separated values for the four longhand transition properties, or you can include a comma-separated list of single transitions. You can't, however, mix the two: transition: transform, opacity 200ms ease-in 50ms will ease in the opacity over 200 milliseconds after a 50-millisecond delay, but the transform change will be instantaneous, with no transitionend event.

Note the duration comes before the delay in all the single transitions. Also note the first single transition omits the delay and timing-function, as the values they're mapped to in the longhand syntax version are the properties' default values.

## In Reverse: Transitioning Back to Baseline

In the preceding examples, we've declared a single transition. All our transitions have been applied in the default state and initiated with a hover. With these declarations, the properties return back to the default state via the same transition on mouseout, with a reversing of the timing function and a duplication of the delay.

With transition declarations only in the global state, both the hover and mouseout states use the same `transition` declaration: the selector matches both states. We can override this duplication of the entire transition or just some of the transition properties by including different values for transition properties in the global (versus the hover-only) state.

When declaring transitions in multiple states, the transition included is *to* that state:

```
a {
    background: yellow;
    transition: 200ms background-color linear 0s;
  }
a:hover {
    background-color: orange;
    /* delay when going <strong>to</strong> the :hover state */
    transition-delay: 50ms;
  }
```

In this scenario, when the user hovers over a link, the background color waits 50 milliseconds before transitioning to orange. When the user mouses off the link, the background starts transitioning back to yellow immediately. In both directions, the transition takes 200 milliseconds to complete, and the gradual change proceeds in a linear manner. The 50 milliseconds is included in the `:hover` (orange) state. The delay happens, therefore, as the background changes to orange. ▶

In our drop-down menu example, on `:hover`, the menu appears and grows over 200 milliseconds, easing in after a delay of 50 milliseconds. The transition is set with the `transition` property in the default (nonhovered) state. When the user mouses out, the properties revert over 200 milliseconds, easing out after a delay of 50 milliseconds. This reverse effect is responding to the `transition` value from the nonhovered state. This is the default behavior, but it's something we can control. The best user experience is this default behavior, so you likely don't want to alter it—but it's important to know that you can.

If we want the closing of the menu to be jumpy and slow (we *don't* want to do that; it's bad user experience. But for the sake of this example, let's pretend we do), we can declare two different transitions:

```
nav ul ul {
  transform: scale(1, 0);
  opacity: 0;
  ...
  transition: all 4s steps(8, start) 1s;
}
nav li:hover ul {
  transform: scale(1, 1);
```

```
    opacity: 1;
    transition: all 200ms linear 50ms;
}
```

Transitions are to the *to* state: when there's a style change, the transition properties used to make the transition are the new values of the transition properties, not the old ones. We put the smooth, linear animation in the :hover state. The transition that applies is the one we are going toward. In the preceding example, when the user hovers over the drop-down menu's parent li, the opening of the drop-down menu will be gradual but quick, lasting 200 milliseconds after a delay of 50 milliseconds. When the user mouses off the drop-down menu or its parent li, the transition will wait one second and take four seconds to complete, showing eight steps along the way.

When we only have one transition, we put it in the global *from* state, as you want the transition to occur toward any state, be that a hovering or a class change. Because we want the transition to occur with any change, we generally put the only transition declaration in the initial, default (least specific) block. If you do want to exert more control and provide for different effects depending on the direction of the transition, make sure to include a transition declaration in all of the possible class and UI states.

Beware of having transitions on both ancestors and descendants. Transitioning properties soon after making a change that transition ancestral or descendant nodes can have unexpected outcomes. If the transition on the descendant completes before the transition on the ancestor, the descendant will then resume inheriting the (still transitioning) value from its parent. This effect may not be what you expected.

# Animatable Properties and Values

Before implementing transitions and animations, it is important to understand what properties are transitionable and animatable. You can transition (or animate) any animatable CSS properties; but which properties are animatable?

While we've included a list of these properties in "Animatable Properties" on page 47, CSS is evolving, and the animatable properties list (*https://developer.mozilla.org/en-US/docs/Web/CSS/CSS_animated_properties*) will likely get new additions.[6]

*Interpolation* is the construction of data points between the values of known data points. The key guideline to determining if a property value is animatable is whether the *computed value* can be interpolated. If a property's keywords are computed values,

---

6 A proposed change to the specifications would make all properties transitionable, even if they aren't in fact animatable. This has yet to be added to the specification, and I don't foresee it being implemented.

they can't be interpolated; if its keywords compute to a number, they can be. The quick rule of thought is that if you can determine a midpoint between two property values, those property values are probably animatable. Values that are interpolatable are animatable. Those that aren't, aren't.

For example, the display values are nonnumeric keywords. Values like block and inline-block aren't numeric and therefore don't have a midpoint; they aren't animatable. The transform property values of rotate(10deg) and rotate(20deg) have a midpoint of rotate(15deg); they are animatable.

The border property is shorthand for border-style, border-width, and border-color (which, in turn, are themselves shorthand properties for the four side values). While there is no midpoint between any of the border-style values, the border-width property length units are numeric, so they can be animated. The keyword values of medium, thick, and thin have numeric equivalents and are interpolatable: the computed value of the border-width property computes those keywords to lengths.

In the border-color value, colors are numeric—the named colors all represent hexadecimal color values—so colors are animatable as well. If you transition from border: red solid 3px to border: blue dashed 10px, the border width and border colors will transition at the defined speed, but border-style will jump from solid to dashed as soon as the new value is applied.

transitionend events will occur for all the animatable properties. In this case, there will be eight transitionend events, for border-top-width, border-right-width, border-bottom-width, border-left-width, border-top-color, border-right-color, border-bottom-color, and border-left-color.

As noted (see Table 2-3), numeric values tend to be animatable. Keyword values that aren't translatable to numeric values generally aren't. CSS functions that take numeric values as parameters generally are animatable. One exception to this rule of thought is visibility: while there is no midpoint between the values of visible and hidden, visibility values are interpolatable between visible and not-visible. When it comes to the visibility property, either the initial value or the destination value must be visible or no interpolation can happen. The value will change at the end of the transition from visible to hidden. For a transition from hidden to visible, it changes at the start of the transition.

auto should generally be considered a nonanimatable value and should be avoided for animations and transitions. According to the specification, it is not an animatable value, but some browsers interpolate the current numeric value of auto (such as height: auto) to be 0px. auto is nonanimatable because it is a computed value for properties like height, width, top, bottom, left, right, and margin.

Often an alternative property or value may work. For example, instead of changing height: 0 to height: auto, use max-height: 0 to max-height: 100vh, which will generally create the expected effect. The auto value is animatable for min-height and min-width, since min-height: auto actually computes to 0.

## How Property Values Are Interpolated

Interpolation can happen when values falling between two or more known values can be determined. Interpolatable values can be transitioned and animated.

Numbers are interpolated as floating-point numbers. Integers are interpolated as whole numbers, incrementing or decrementing as whole numbers.

In CSS, length and percentage units are translated into real numbers. When transitioning or animating calc(), or from one type of length to or from a percentage, the values will be converted into a calc() function and interpolated as real numbers.

Colors, whether they are HSLA, RGB, or named colors, are interpolated into their RGBA equivalent values for transitioning.

When animating font weights, if you use keyterms like bold, they'll be converted to numeric values and animated in steps of multiples of 100. You may be used to writing bold and normal, but the values of 100 through 900 have been around as long as CSS—since CSS Level 1 in 1996.

When including animatable property values that have more than one component, each component is interpolated appropriately for that component. For example, text-shadow has up to four components: the color, x, y, and blur. The color is interpolated as color: the x, y, and blur components are interpolated as lengths. Box shadows have two additional optional properties: inset (or lack thereof) and spread. spread, being a length, is interpolated as such. The inset keyterm cannot be converted to a numeric equivalent: you can transition from one inset shadow to another inset shadow, or from one drop shadow to another drop shadow multi-component value, but there is no way to gradually transition between inset and drop shadows.

Similar to values with more than one component, gradients can be transitioned only if you are transitioning gradients of the same type (linear or radial) with equal numbers of color stops. The colors of each color stop are then interpolated as colors, and the position of each color stop is interpolated as length and percentage units.

## Repeating values

When you have simple lists of other types of properties, each item in the list is interpolated appropriately for that type—as long as the lists have the same number of
items or repeatable items, and each pair of values can be interpolated:

```
.img {
    background-image:
        url(1.gif), url(2.gif), url(3.gif), url(4.gif),
        url(5.gif), url(6.gif), url(7.gif), url(8.gif),
        url(9.gif), url(10.gif), url(11.gif), url(12.gif);
    background-size: 10px 10px, 20px 20px, 30px 30px, 40px 40px;
    transition: background-size 1s ease-in 0s;
}
.img:hover {
    background-size: 25px 25px, 50px 50px, 75px 75px, 100px 100px;
}
```

For example, in transitioning four background-sizes, with all the sizes in both lists listed in pixels, the third background-size from the pretransitioned state can gradually
transition to the third background-size of the transitioned list. In the preceding
example, background images 1, 6, and 10 will transition from 10px to 25px in height
and width when hovered. Similarly, images 3, 7, and 11 will transition from 30px to
75px, and so forth.

Remember, when there aren't enough declarations to match the number of background layers, the values are repeated. If there are too many values, the excess values
are ignored. In this case, the background-size values are repeated three times, as if
the CSS had been written as:

```
.img {
    ...
    background-size: 10px 10px, 20px 20px, 30px 30px, 40px 40px,
                     10px 10px, 20px 20px, 30px 30px, 40px 40px,
                     10px 10px, 20px 20px, 30px 30px, 40px 40px;
    ...
}
.img:hover {
    background-size: 25px 25px, 50px 50px, 75px 75px, 100px 100px,
                     25px 25px, 50px 50px, 75px 75px, 100px 100px,
                     25px 25px, 50px 50px, 75px 75px, 100px 100px;
}
```

If a property doesn't have enough comma-separated values to match the number of
background images, the list of values is repeated until there are enough, even when
the list in the :hover state doesn't match the initial state:

```
.img:hover {
    background-size: 33px 33px, 66px 66px, 99px 99px;
}
```

If we transitioned from four `background-size` declarations in the initial state to three `background-size` declarations in the :hover state, all in pixels, still with 12 background images, the hover and initial state values are repeated (three and four times respectively) until we have the 12 necessary values, as if the following had been declared:

```
.img {
    ...
    background-size: 10px 10px, 20px 20px, 30px 30px,
                     40px 40px, 10px 10px, 20px 20px,
                     30px 30px, 40px 40px, 10px 10px,
                     20px 20px, 30px 30px, 40px 40px;
    ...
}
.img:hover {
    background-size: 33px 33px, 66px 66px, 99px 99px,
                     33px 33px, 66px 66px, 99px 99px,
                     33px 33px, 66px 66px, 99px 99px,
                     33px 33px, 66px 66px, 99px 99px;
}
```

If a pair of values cannot be interpolated—for example, if the `background-size` changes from `contain` in the default state to `cover` when hovered—then, according to the specification, the lists are not interpolatable. However, some browsers ignore that particular pair of values for the purposes of the transition, but still animate the interpolatable values.

There are some property values that can animate if the browser can infer implicit values. For example, shadows. For shadows, the browser will infer an implicit shadow `box-shadow: transparent 0 0 0` or `box-shadow: inset transparent 0 0 0`, replacing any values not explicitly included in the pre- or post-transition state. These examples are in the chapter files for this book (*http://www.standardista.com/css3/tran sitions*).

Only the interpolatable values lead to `transitionend` events.

As noted previously, `visibility` animates differently than other properties: if animating or transitioning to or from `visible`, it is interpolated as a discrete step. It is always visible during the transition or animation as long as the timing function output is between 0 and 1. It will switch at the beginning if the transition is from `hidden` to `visible`. It will switch at the end if the transition is from `visible` to `hidden`. Note that this can be controlled with the step timing functions.

# Animatable Properties

There is a list of animatable properties in the CSS Transitions specification (*http://dev.w3.org/csswg/css-transitions/#animatable-properties*). This list only lists the CSS 2.1 properties that are transitionable, so it is not wholly accurate.

Table 2-3 shows a list of animatable properties and how their values are interpolated.

*Table 2-3. Animatable properties*

| | Property name | Interpolation | |
|---|---|---|---|
| **COLOR** | | | |
| | color | as color | |
| | opacity | as number | |
| **COLUMNS** | | | |
| | column-width | as length | |
| | column-count | as integer | |
| | column-gap | as length | |
| | column-rule (see longhands) | | |
| | column-rule-color: | as color | |
| | column-rule-style: | no | |
| | column-rule-width: | as length | |
| | break-before | no | |
| | break-after | no | |
| | break-inside | no | |
| | column-span | no | |
| | column-fill | no | |
| **TEXT** | | | |
| | hyphens | no | |
| | letter-spacing | as length | |
| | word-wrap | no | |
| | overflow-wrap | no | |
| | text-transform | no | |
| | tab-size | as length | |
| | text-align | no | |

| Property name | Interpolation |
|---|---|
| text-align-last | no |
| text-indent | as length, percentage, or calc(); |
| direction | no |
| white-space | no |
| word-break | no |
| word-spacing | as length |
| line-break | no |

## TEXT DECORATIONS

| | |
|---|---|
| text-decoration-color: | as color |
| text-decoration-style: | no |
| text-decoration-line: | no |
| text-decoration-skip | no |
| text-shadow | as shadow list |
| text-underline-position | no |

## FLEXIBLE BOXES

| | |
|---|---|
| align-content | no |
| align-items | no |
| align-self | no |
| flex-basis | as length, percentage, or calc(); |
| flex-direction | no |
| flex-flow | no |
| flex (see longhand) | |
| flex-grow | as number |
| flex-shrink | as number |
| flex-basis: | as length, percentage, or calc(); |
| flex-wrap | no |
| justify-content | no |
| order | as integer |

## BACKGROUND AND BORDERS

| | |
|---|---|
| background | |
| background-color: | as color |
| background-image: | no |

| Property name | Interpolation |
|---|---|
| background-clip: | no |
| background-position: | as list of length, percentage, or calc |
| background-size: | as list of length, percentage, or calc |
| background-repeat: | no |
| background-attachment | no |
| abackground-origin | no |

## BORDERS

| | |
|---|---|
| border (see longhand) | |
| border-color | as color |
| border-style | no |
| border-width | as length |
| border-radius | as length, percentage, or calc(); |
| border-image | no (see longhand) |
| border-image-outset | no |
| border-image-repeat | no |
| border-image-slice | no |
| border-image-source | no |
| border-image-width | no |

## BOX MODEL

| | |
|---|---|
| box-decoration-break | no |
| box-shadow | as shadow list |
| margin | as length |
| padding | as length |
| box-sizing | no |
| max-height | as length, percentage, or calc(); |
| min-height | as length, percentage, or calc(); |
| height | as length, percentage, or calc(); |
| max-width | as length, percentage, or calc(); |
| min-width | as length, percentage, or calc(); |
| width | as length, percentage, or calc(); |
| overflow | no |
| visibility | as visibility (see "How Property Values Are Interpolated" on page 44) |

| Property name | Interpolation |
|---|---|
| **TABLE** | |
| border-collapse | no |
| border-spacing | no |
| caption-side | no |
| empty-cells | no |
| table-layout | no |
| vertical-align | as length |
| **POSITIONING** | |
| bottom | as length, percentage, or calc(); |
| left | as length, percentage, or calc(); |
| right | as length, percentage, or calc(); |
| top | as length, percentage, or calc(); |
| float | no |
| clear | no |
| position | no |
| z-index | as integer |
| **FONTS** | |
| font (see longhand) | |
| font-style | no |
| font-variant | no |
| font-weight | as font weight |
| font-stretch | as font stretch |
| font-size | as length |
| line-height | as number, length |
| font-family | no |
| font-variant-ligatures | no |
| font-feature-settings | no |
| font-language-override | no |
| font-size-adjust | as number |
| font-synthesis | no |
| font-kerning | no |
| font-variant-position | no |

| Property name | Interpolation |
| --- | --- |
| font-variant-caps | no |
| font-variant-numeric | no |
| font-variant-east-asian | no |
| font-variant-alternates | no |

## IMAGES

| | |
| --- | --- |
| object-fit | no |
| object-position | as length, percentage, or calc(); |
| image-rendering | no |
| image-orientation | no |

## COUNTERS, LISTS, AND GENERATED CONTENT

| | |
| --- | --- |
| content | no |
| quotes | no |
| counter-increment | no |
| counter-reset | no |
| list-style | no |
| list-style-image | no |
| list-style-position | no |
| list-style-type | no |

## PAGE

| | |
| --- | --- |
| orphans | no |
| page-break-after | no |
| page-break-before | no |
| page-break-inside | no |
| widows | no |

## USER INTERFACE

| | |
| --- | --- |
| outline (see longhand) | |
| outline-color | as color |
| outline-width | as length |
| outline-style | no |
| outline-offset | as length |
| cursor | no |

| Property name | Interpolation |
|---|---|
| resize | no |
| text-overflow | no |

## ANIMATIONS

| Property name | Interpolation |
|---|---|
| animation | no (see longhands) |
| animation-delay | no |
| animation-direction | no |
| animation-duration | no |
| animation-fill-mode | no |
| animation-iteration-count | no |
| animation-name | no |
| animation-play-state | no |
| animation-timing-function | no, though animation-timing-function can be included in keyframes |

## TRANSITIONS

| Property name | Interpolation |
|---|---|
| transition | no (see longhands) |
| transition-delay | no |
| transition-duration | no |
| transition-property | no |
| transition-timing-function | no |

## TRANSFORM PROPERTIES

| Property name | Interpolation |
|---|---|
| transform | as transform (see *Transforms in CSS* [O'Reilly]) |
| transform-origin | as length, percentage or calc(); |
| transform-style | no |
| perspective | as length |
| perspective-origin | as simple list of a length, percentage or calc(); |
| backface-visibility | no |

## COMPOSITING AND BLENDING

| Property name | Interpolation |
|---|---|
| background-blend-mode | no |
| mix-blend-mode | no |
| isolation | no |

| | Property name | Interpolation |
|---|---|---|
| **SHAPES** | | |
| | shape-outside | yes, as basic-shape |
| | shape-margin | as length, percentage, or calc(); |
| | shape-image-threshold | as number |
| **MISCELLANEOUS** | | |
| | clip (deprecated) | as rectangle |
| | display | no |
| | unicode-bidi | no |
| | text-orientation | no |
| | ime-mode | no |
| | all | as each of the properties of the shorthand (all properties but unicode-bidi and direction) |
| | will-change | no |
| | box-decoration-break | no |
| | touch-action | no |
| | initial-letter | no |
| | initial-letter-align | no |

# transition Events Revisited

The transitionend event fires when a transition completes.

The transitionend event has three properties. propertyName is the name of the CSS property whose transition completed, and elapsedTime is the number of seconds the transition had been running at the time the event fired, not including the transition delay. The third property is the pseudoElement property, which returns the name of the pseudo-element on which the transition occurred, either ::before or ::after (with two colons), or the empty string if the transition occurred on an element and not a pseudo-element.

Currently, the transitionend event will only occur if there is a positive, nonzero transition-delay or a nonzero transition-duration. The transitionend event only occurs if the sum of transition-delay (which can be negative) and transition-duration (which can't) is greater than zero. If there is no delay or no duration, there is no gradual transition, and no transitionend is fired, even if a property value has changed state.

You can use the `addEventListener()` method for the `transitionend` event to listen for this event.

If a keyframe animation, explained in the next chapter, is applied to a transitioning element, and it animates the same properties that are being transitioned, the animation takes precedence over the transition. Oddly, the `transitionend` event will still occur, but it will occur at the end of the animation.

### Printing transitions

When web pages or web applications are printed, the stylesheet for print media is used. If your style element's media attribute matches only `screen`, the CSS will not impact the printed page at all.

Often, no media attribute is included; it is as if `media="all"` were set, which is the default. Depending on the browser, when a transitioned element is printed, either the interpolating values are ignored, or the property values in their current state are printed.

You can't see the element transitioning on a piece of paper, but in some browsers, like Chrome, if an element transitioned from one state to another, the current state at the time the `print` function is called will be the value on the printed page, if that property is printable. For example, if a background color changed, neither the pre-transition or the post-transition background color will be printed, as background colors are generally not printed. However, if the text color mutated from one value to another, the current value of `color` will be what gets printed on a color printer or PDF.

In other browsers, like Firefox, whether the pre-transition or post-transition value is printed depends on how the transition was initiated. If it initiated with a hover, the non-hovered value will be printed, as you are no longer hovering over the element while you interact with the print dialog. If it transitioned with a class addition, the post-transition value will be printed, even if the transition hasn't completed. The printing acts as if the transition properties are ignored.

Given that there are separate printstyle sheets or @media rules for print, browsers compute style separately. In the print style, styles don't change, so there just aren't any transitions. The printing acts as if the property values changed instantly, instead of transitioning over time.

# CHAPTER 3

# Animation

CSS transitions, covered in the previous chapter, enabled simple animations. With transitions, an element's properties change from the values set in one style block to the values set in a different style block as the element changes state over time instead of instantly. With CSS transitions, the start and end states of property values are controlled by existing property values and provide little control over how the property value interpolation progresses over time.

CSS animations are similar to transitions in that values of CSS properties change over time. But transitions only let us animate from an initial value to a destination value and back again. CSS keyframe animations let us decide if and how an animation repeats and give us granular control over what happens throughout the animation.

CSS animation lets us animate the values of CSS properties over time using keyframes. Similar to transitions, animation provides us with control over the delay and duration. With CSS animations, we can control the number of iterations, the iteration behavior, what happens before the first animation commences, and the state of animated properties after the last animation iteration concludes. CSS animation properties allow us to control timing and even pause an animation mid-stream.

While transitions trigger implicit property values changes, animations are explicitly executed when animation keyframe properties are applied.

With CSS animations, you can change property values that are not part of the set pre or post state of the element. The property values set on the animated element don't necessarily have to be part of the animation progression. For example, with transitions, going from black to white will only display varying shades of gray. With animation, that same element doesn't have to be black or white or even in-between shades of gray during the animation. While you *can* transition through shades of gray, you could instead turn the element yellow, then animate from yellow to orange.

Alternatively, you could animate through various colors, starting with black and ending with white, but progressing through the entire rainbow ▶[1] if you so choose. With animations, you can use as many keyframes as needed to granularly control an element's property values to create your desired effect.

The first step in implementing CSS animations is to create a *keyframe animation*—a reusable @keyframes at-rule defining which properties will be animated and how. The second step is to apply that keyframe animation to one or more elements in your document or application, using various animation properties to define how it will progress through the keyframes.

## Keyframes

To animate an element, we need to set the name of a keyframe animation; to do that, we need a named keyframe animation. Our first step is to define this reusable CSS keyframe animation using the @keyframes at-rule.

To define a CSS animation, we declare a reusable keyframe animation using the @keyframes rule, giving our animation a name. The name we create will then be used within a CSS selector's code block to attach this particular animation to the element(s) and/or pseudo-element(s) defined by the selector(s).

The @keyframes at-rule includes the animation identifier, or name, and one or more keyframe blocks. Each keyframe block includes one or more keyframe selectors with declaration blocks of zero or more property/value pairs. The entire @keyframes at-rule specifies the behavior of one full iteration of the animation. The animation may iterate zero or more times, depending mainly on the animation-iteration-count property value, which we'll discuss in "The animation-iteration-count Property" on page 68.

The @keyframes at-rule keyterm is followed by the *animation_identifier* (the name you give your animation for future reference), followed by curly braces that encompass the series of keyframe blocks.

Each keyframe block includes one or more keyframe selectors. The keyframe selectors are percentage-of-time positions along the duration of the animation; they are declared either as percentages or with the keyterms from or to:

```
@keyframes animation_identifier {
  keyframe_selectorA {
    property1: value1a;
    property2: value2b;
  }
```

---

1 All of the examples in this chapter can be found at *http://standardista.com/css3/animations*.

---

```
    keyframe_selectorB {
      property1: value1b;
      property2: value2b;
    }
  }
```

# Setting Up Your Keyframe Animation

To create our keyframe animation, we start with the @keyframes at-rule keyterm, an animation name, and curly brackets to encompass the animation directives. Within the opening and closing curly brackets, we include a series of keyframe selectors with blocks of CSS in which we declare the properties we want to animate. The keyframes we declare don't in themselves animate anything. Rather, we must attach the keyframe animations we created via the animation-name property, whose value is the name or animation identifier we provided within our at-rule. We discuss that property in "The animation-name Property" on page 64.

Start with the at-rule declaration, followed by the animation name and brackets:

```
@keyframes nameOfAnimation {
  ...
}
```

The name, which you create, is an identifier, not a string. Identifiers have specific rules. First, they can't be quoted. You can use any characters [a-zA-Z0-9], the hyphen (-), underscore (_), and any ISO 10646 character U+00A0 and higher. ISO 10646 is the universal character set; this means you can use any character in the Unicode standard that matches the regular expression [-_a-zA-Z0-9\u00A0-\u10FFFF].

There are some limitations on the name. As mentioned, do not quote the animation identifier (or animation name). ⊙ The name can't start with a digit [0-9] or two hyphens. One hyphen is fine, as long as it is not followed by a digit—unless you escape the digit or hyphen with a backslash.

If you include any escape characters within your animation name, make sure to escape them with a backslash (\). For example, Q&A! must be written as Q\&A\!. âœŽ can be left as âœŽ (no, that's not a typo), and ✎ is a valid name as well. But if you are going to use any keyboard characters that aren't letters or digits, like !, @, #, $, %, ^, &, *, (, ), +, =, ~, \\, ,, ., ', ", ;, :, [, ], {, }, |, \, or /, escape them with a backslash.

Also, don't use any of the keyterms covered in this chapter as the name of your animation. For example, possible values for the various animation properties we'll be covering later in the chapter include none, paused, running, infinite, backwards, and forwards, among others. Using an animation property keyterm, while not prohibited by the spec, will likely break your animation ⊙ when using the animation shorthand property discussed in "The animation Shorthand Property" on page 99.

So, while you can legally name your animation paused (or another keyterm,) I strongly recommend against it:

```
@keyframes bouncing {
    ...
}
```

After declaring the name of our @keyframe animation, in this case bouncing, we enclose all the rules of our at-rule in curly braces, as shown in the last code snippet. This is where we will put all our keyframes.

# Keyframe Selectors

Keyframe selectors provide points during our animation where we set the values of the properties we want to animate. In defining animations, we dictate the values we want properties to have at a specific percentage of the way through the animations. If you want a value at the start of the animation, you declare it at the 0% mark. If you want a different value at the end of the animation, you declare the property value at the 100% mark. If you want a value a third of the way through the animation, you declare it at the 33% mark. These marks are defined with keyframe selectors.

Keyframe selectors consist of a comma-separated list of one or more percentage values or the keywords from or to. The keyword from is equal to 0%. The keyword to equals 100%. The keyframe selectors are used to specify the percentage along the duration of the animation the keyframe represents. The keyframe itself is specified by the block of property values declared on the selector. The % unit must be used on percentage values: in other words, 0 is invalid as a keyframe selector:

```
@keyframes W {
    from {
      left: 0;
      top: 0;
    }
    25%, 75% {
      top: 100%;
    }
    50% {
      top: 50%;
    }
    to {
      left: 100%;
      top: 0;
    }
}
```

This @keyframes animation, named W, when attached to a non-statically positioned element, would move that element along a W-shaped path. W has five keyframes, at the 0%, 25%, 50%, 75%, and 100% marks. The from is the 0% mark. The to is the 100% mark. ⓑ

As the property values we set for the 25% and 75% mark are the same, we put two key-frame selectors together as a comma-separated list. Just as with regular CSS selectors, we can put multiple comma-separated keyframe selectors together in front of a single CSS block. Whether you keep those selectors on one line (as in the example) or put each selector on its own line is up to your own CSS style guidelines:

```
25%,
75% {
   top: 100%;
}
```

Note that selectors do not need to be listed in ascending order. In the preceding example, we've placed the 25% and 75% on the same line, with the 50% mark coming after that declaration. For legibility, it is highly encouraged to progress from the 0% to the 100% mark. However, as demonstrated by the 75% keyframe in this example, which is "out of order," it is not required.

## Omitting from and to Values

If a 0% or from keyframe is not specified, then the user agent (browser) constructs a 0% keyframe using the original values of the properties being animated, as if the 0% keyframe were declared with the same property values that impact the element when no animation was applied. Similarly, if the 100% or to keyframe is not defined, the browser creates a faux 100% keyframe using the value the element would have had if no animation had been set on it.

Assuming we have a background-color change animation:

```
@keyframes change_bgcolor {
    45% { background-color: green; }
    55% { background-color: blue; }
}
```

And the element originally had background-color: red set on it, it would be as if the animation were written as: ⓑ

```
@keyframes change_bgcolor {
    0%   { background-color: red; }
    45%  { background-color: green; }
    55%  { background-color: blue; }
    100% { background-color: red; }
}
```

Or, remembering that we can include multiple identical keyframes as a comma-separated list, this faux animation could have also been written as:

```
@keyframes change_bgcolor {
    0%,
    100% { background-color: red; }
    45% { background-color: green; }
    55% { background-color: blue; }
}
```

Note the `background-color: red;` declarations are not actually part of the keyframe animation. If the background color were set to yellow in the element's default state, the `0%` and `100%` marks would display a yellow background, animating into green, then blue, then back to yellow as the animation progressed:

```
@keyframes change_bgcolor {
    0%, 100% { background-color: yellow; }
    45% { background-color: green; }
    55% { background-color: blue; }
}
```

We can include this `change_bgcolor` animation on many elements, and the perceived animation will differ based on the element's value for the `background-color` property in the nonanimated state.

Negative percentages, values greater than `100%`, and values that aren't otherwise percentages or the keyterms `to` or `from` are not valid and will be ignored. Noninteger percentage values, such as `33.33%`, are valid.

## Repeating Keyframe Properties

In the original `-webkit-` implementation of animation, each keyframe could only be declared once: if declared more than once, only the last declaration would be applied, and the previous keyframe selector block was ignored. This has been updated. Now, similar to the rest of CSS, the values in the keyframe declaration blocks with identical keyframe values cascade. In the standard (nonprefixed) syntax, the preceding W animation can be written with the `to`, or `100%`, declared twice, overriding the value of the left property:

```
@keyframes W {
    from, to {
        top: 0;
        left: 0;
    }
    25%, 75% {
        top: 100%;
    }
    50% {
        top: 50%;
    }
```

```
    to {
      left: 100%;
    }
  }
```

Note that in the preceding code block, `to` is declared along with `from` as keyframe selectors for the first code block. The `left` value is overridden for the `to` in the last keyframe block.

## Animatable Properties

Not all properties are animatable. Similar to the rest of CSS, the browser ignores properties and values in a keyframe declaration block that are not understood. Properties that are not animatable, with the exception of `animation-timing-function`, are also ignored. There is a fairly exhaustive list of animatable properties maintained by the community on the Mozilla Developer Network (*https://developer.mozilla.org/en-US/docs/Web/CSS/CSS_animated_properties*) site.

> The `animation-timing-function`, described in greater detail in "The `animation-timing-function` Property" on page 83, while not an animatable property, is not ignored. If you include the `animation-timing-function` as a keyframe style rule within a keyframe selector block, the timing function of the properties within that block will change to the declared timing function when the animation moves to the next keyframe.

You should not try to animate between nonnumeric values, with a few exceptions. For example, you can animate between nonnumeric values as long as they can be extrapolated into a numeric value, like named colors, which are extrapolated to hexadecimal color values.

If the animation is set between two property values that don't have a midpoint, the results may not be what you expect: the property will not animate correctly—or at all. For example, you shouldn't declare an element's height to animate between `height: auto` and `height: 300px`. There is no midpoint between `auto` and `300px`. The element may still animate, but different browsers handle this differently: Firefox does not animate the element; Safari may animate as if `auto` is equal to `0`; and both Opera and Chrome currently jump from the preanimated state to the postanimated state halfway through the animation, which may or may not be at the `50%` keyframe selector, depending on the value of the `animation-timing-function`. In other words, different browsers behave differently for different properties when there is no midpoint, so you can't be sure you will get your expected outcome.

The behavior of your animation will be most predictable if you declare both a 0% and a 100% value for every property you animate. ⊙

```
@keyframes round {
    100% {
        border-radius: 50%;
    }
}
```

For example, if you declare `border-radius: 50%;` in your animation, you may want to declare `border-radius: 0;` as well, because there is no midpoint between none and anything: the default value of `border-radius` is none, not 0:

```
@keyframes square_to_round {
    0% {
        border-radius: 0%;
    }
    100% {
        border-radius: 50%;
    }
}
```

The `round` animation will animate an element using the original `border-radius` value of that element to a `border-radius` of 50% over the duration of the animation cycle. The `round` animation may work as expected if you are turning rounded corner buttons into ovals (but it isn't likely to look good).

While including a `0%` keyframe will ensure that your animation runs smoothly, the element may have had rounded corners to begin with. By adding `border-radius: 0%;` in the `from` keyframe, if the element was originally rounded, it will jump to rectangular corners before it starts animating. This might not be what you want. The best way to resolve this issue is to use the `round` animation instead of `square_to_round`, making sure any element that gets animated with the `round` keyframe animation has its `border-radius` explicitly set. ⊙

As long as an animatable property is included in at least one block with a value that is different then the nonanimated attribute value, and there is a possible midpoint between those two values, that property will animate.

## Nonanimatable Properties That Aren't Ignored

Exceptions to the midpoint "rule" include `visibility` and `animation-timing-function`.

`Visibility` is an animatable property, even though there is no midpoint between `visibility: hidden` and `visibility: visible`. When you animate from hidden to visible, the visibility value jumps from one value to the next at the keyframe upon which it is declared.

While the `animation-timing-function` is not, in fact, an animatable property, when included in a keyframe block, the animation timing will switch to the newly declared value at that point in the animation for the properties within that keyframe selector block. The change in animation timing is not animated; it simply switches to the new value.

## Dynamically Changing @keyframes Animations

There is an API that enables finding, appending, and deleting keyframe rules. You can change the content of a keyframe block within an @keyframes animation declaration with `appendRule(n)` or `deleteRule(n)`, where n is the full selector of that keyframe. You can return the contents of a keyframe with `findRule(n)`:

```
@keyframes W {
  from, to {
    top: 0;
    left: 0;
  }
  25%, 75% {
    top: 100%;
  }
  50% {
    top: 50%;
  }
  to {
    left: 100%;
  }
}
```

The `appendRule()`, `deleteRule()`, and `findRule()` methods takes the full keyframe selector as an argument. Revisiting the W animation, to return the 25% / 75% keyframe, the argument is 25%, 75%:

```
// Get the selector and content block for a keyframe
var aRule = myAnimation.findRule('25%, 75%').cssText;

// Delete the 50% keyframe rule
myAnimation.deleteRule('50%');

// Add a 53% keyframe rules to the end of the animation
myAnimation.appendRule('53% {top: 50%;}');
```

The statement `myAnimation.findRule('25%, 75%').cssText;` where `myAnimation` is pointing to a keyframe animation, returns the keyframe that matches 25%, 75%. It would not match anything if we had used either 25% or 75% only. If pointing to the W animation, this statement returns 25%, 75% { top: 100%; }.

Similarly, `myAnimation.deleteRule('50%')` will delete the last 50% keyframe. `deleteRule(n)` deletes the last keyframe rule that has a keyframe selector n. To add a keyframe, `myAnimation.appendRule('53% {top: 50%;}')` will append a 53% keyframe after the last keyframe of the @keyframes block. ▶

# Animated Elements

Once you have created a keyframe animation, you need to apply that animation to elements and/or pseudo-elements for anything to actually animate. CSS animation provides us with numerous animation properties to attach a keyframe animation to an element and control its progression. At a minimum, we need to include the name of the animation for the element to animate, and a duration if we want the animation to actually be visible.

There are three animation events—`animationstart`, `animationend`, and `animationiteration`—that occur at the start and end of an animation, and between the end of an iteration and the start of a subsequent iteration. Any animation for which a valid keyframe rule is defined will generate the start and end events, even animations with empty keyframe rules. The `animationiteration` event only occurs when an animation has more than one iteration, as the `animationiteration` event does not fire if the `animationend` event would fire at the same time.

There are two ways of attaching animation properties to an element: you can include all the animation properties separately, or you can declare all the properties in one line using the `animation` shorthand property (or a combination of shorthand and longhand properties). We are going to first learn all the longhand properties. Later in this chapter, we'll condense all the declarations into one line with the `animation` shorthand property.

Let's start with the individual properties:

## The `animation-name` Property

The `animation-name` property takes as its value the name or comma-separated list of names of the keyframe animation you want to apply to an element or group of elements. The names are the unquoted identifiers you created in your @keyframes rule.

---

### `animation-name`

| | |
|---|---|
| **Values:** | `<@keyframes_identifier>`\|`none`\|`inherit`\|`initial` |
| **Initial value:** | `none` |
| **Applies to:** | All elements, `::before` and `::after` pseudo-elements |
| **Inherited:** | No |

---

The default value is none, which means there is no animation. The none value can be used to override any animation applied elsewhere in the CSS cascade. (This is also the reason you don't want to name your animation none, unless you're a masochist.) To apply an animation, include the @keyframe identifier, which is the animation name. ⓟ

Using the change_bgcolor keyframe animation defined in "Omitting from and to Values" on page 59:

```
div {
    animation-name: change_bgcolor;
}
```

To apply more than one animation, include more than one comma-separated @keyframe identifier:

```
div {
    animation-name: change_bgcolor, round, W;
}
```

If one of the included keyframe identifiers does not exist, the series of animations will not fail: rather, the failed animation will be ignored, and the valid animations will be applied. While ignored initially, the failed animation will be applied if and when that identifier comes into existence as a valid animation:

```
div {
    animation-name: change_bgcolor, spin, round, W;
}
```

In this example, there is no spin keyframe animation defined. The spin animation will be ignored, while the change_bgcolor, round, and W animations are applied. Should a spin keyframe animation come into existence, it will be applied to the element at that time.

In order to include more than one animation, we've included each @keyframe animation identifier in our list of comma-separated values on the animation-name property. If more than one animation is applied to an element and those animations have repeated properties, the latter animations override the property values in the preceding animations. For example, if more than two background color changes are applied concurrently in two different keyframe animations, the latter animation will override the background property declarations of the preceding one, but only if the background colors were set to change at the same time. For more on this, see "Animation, Specificity, and Precedence Order" on page 102. ⓟ

While not required, if you include three animation names, consider including three values for all the animation longhand property values, such as animation-duration and animation-iteration-count, so there are corresponding values for each attached animation. If there are too many values, the extra values are ignored. If there are too few comma-separated values, the provided values will be repeated. In other words, while it often makes sense to include the same number of values for each animation property as you do for the animation-name property, including fewer or more valid values will not invalidate the animations.

 If an included keyframe identifier doesn't exist, the animation doesn't fail. Any other animations attached via the animation-name property will proceed normally. If that nonexistent animation comes into existence, the animation will be attached to the element when the identifier becomes valid, and will start iterating immediately or after the expiration of any animation-delay. See "Setting Up Your Keyframe Animation" on page 57. ▶

This is true as long as the keyframe identifier for the nonexistent animation is a valid identifier. change_bgcolor, spin, round, W will work in spite of there being no spin animation, but change_bgcolor, Q&A!, round, W would fail, even if a Q&A! animation is declared, as Q&A! is not a valid identifier.

Simply applying an animation to an element is not enough for the element to visibly animate, but it will make the animation occur. The keyframe properties will be interpolated, and the animationstart and animationend events will fire. A single animationstart event occurs when the animation starts, and a single animationend event occurs when the animation ends, because the property-value interpolation occurs even if there was no perceptible animation.

For an element to visibly animate, the animation must last at least some amount of time. For that we have the animation-duration property.

## The animation-duration Property

The animation-duration property defines how long a single animation iteration should take in seconds (s) or milliseconds (ms).

The animation-duration property takes as its value the length of time, in seconds (s) or milliseconds (ms), it should take to complete one cycle through all the keyframes. If omitted, the animation will still be applied with a duration of 0s, with animation start and animationend still being fired even though the animation, taking 0s, is imperceptible. Negative values are invalid.

When including a duration, you must include the second (s) or millisecond (ms) unit:

```
div {
    animation-name: change_bgcolor;
    animation-duration: 200ms;
}
```

# animation-duration

**Values:**         <time>

**Initial value:**  0s

**Applies to:**     All elements, ::before and ::after pseudo-elements

**Inherited:**      No

If you have more than one animation, you can include a different animation-duration for each animation by including more than one comma-separated time duration:

```
div {
    animation-name: change_bgcolor, round, W;
    animation-duration: 200ms, 100ms, 0.5s;
}
```

If you have an invalid value within your comma-separated list of durations, like animation-duration: 200ms, 0, 0.5s, the entire declaration will fail, and it will behave as if animation-duration: 0s had been declared. 0 is not a valid time value. ▶

Generally, you will want to include an animation-duration value for each animation-name provided. If you have only one duration, all the animations will last the same amount of time. Having fewer animation-duration values than animation-name values in your comma-separated property value list will not fail: rather, the values that are included will be repeated. If you have a greater number of animation-duration values than animation-name values, the extra values will be ignored. If one of the included animations does not exist, the series of animations and animation durations will not fail: the failed animation, along with its duration, are ignored:

```
div {
    animation-name: change_bgcolor, spin, round, W;
    animation-duration: 200ms, 5s, 100ms, 0.5s;
}
```

In this example, the 5s, or 5 seconds, is associated with `spin`. As there is no `spin` @keyframes declaration, `spin` doesn't exist, and the 5s and `spin` are ignored. Should a spin animation come into existence, it will be applied to the `div` and last 5 seconds.

## The `animation-iteration-count` Property

Simply including the required `animation-name` will lead to the animation playing once. Include the `animation-iteration-count` property if you want to iterate through the animation more or less than the default one time.

---

### animation-iteration-count

**Values:** `<number> | infinite | initial`

**Initial value:** 1

**Applies to:** All elements, `::before` and `::after` pseudo-elements

**Inherited:** No

---

By default, the animation will occur once. If `animation-iteration-count` is included, and there isn't a negative value for the `animation-delay` property, the animation will repeat the number of times specified by the value if the property, which can be any number or the keyterm `infinite`.

If the numeric value is not an integer, the animation will end partway through its last cycle. The animation will still run, but will cut off mid-iteration on the final iteration. For example, `animation-iteration-count: 1.25` will iterate through the animation 1.25 times, cutting off 25% through the second iteration. If the value is `0.25` on an 8-second animation, the animation will play about 25% of the way through, ending after 2 seconds.

Negative numbers are not valid. Like any invalid value, a negative value will lead to a default single iteration. ▶

Interestingly, `0` is a valid value for the `animation-iteration-count` property. When set to `0`, the animation still occurs, but zero times. It is similar to setting `animation-duration: 0s`: it will throw both an `animationstart` and an `animationend` event.

If you are attaching more than one animation to an element or pseudo-element, include a comma-separated list of values for `animation-name`, `animation-duration`, and `animation-iteration-count`:

```
.flag {
    animation-name: red, white, blue;
    animation-duration: 2s, 4s, 6s;
    animation-iteration-count: 3, 5;
}
```

The `iteration-count` values (and all other animation property values) will be assigned in the order of the comma-separated `animation-name` property value. Extra values will be ignored. Missing values will cause the existing values to be repeated. Invalid values will invalidate the entire declaration.

In the preceding example, there are more name values than count values, so the count values will repeat: `red` and `blue` will iterate three times, and `white` will iterate five times. There are the same number of name values as duration values; therefore, the duration values will not repeat. The `red` animation lasts two seconds, iterating three times, and therefore will run for six seconds. The `white` animation lasts four seconds, iterating five times, for a total of 20 seconds. The `blue` animation is six seconds per iteration with the repeated three iterations value, animating for a total of 18 seconds.

If we wanted all three animations to end at the same time, even though their durations differ, we can control that with `animation-iteration-count`:

```
.flag {
    animation-name: red, white, blue;
    animation-duration: 2s, 4s, 6s;
    animation-iteration-count: 6, 3, 2;
}
```

In that example, the `red`, `white`, and `blue` animations will last for a total of 12 seconds each: `red` animates over 2 seconds, iterating 6 times, for a total of 12 seconds; `white` lasts 4 seconds, iterating 3 times, for a total of 12 seconds; and `blue` lasts 6 seconds, iterating 2 times, for a total of 12 seconds. With simple arithmetic, you can figure out how many iterations you need to make one effect last as long as another, remembering that the `animation-iteration-count` value doesn't need to be an integer.

## The `animation-direction` Property

With the `animation-direction` property, you can control whether the animation progresses from the 0% keyframe to the 100% keyframe, or from the 100% keyframe to the 0% keyframe. You can control whether all the iterations progress in the same direction, or set every other animation cycle to progress in the opposite direction.

## animation-direction

| | |
|---|---|
| **Values:** | normal \| reverse \| alternate \| alternate-reverse |
| **Initial value:** | normal |
| **Applies to:** | All elements, ::before and ::after pseudo-elements |
| **Inherited:** | No |

The animation-direction property defines the direction of the animation's progression through the keyframes. There are four possible values:

animation-direction: normal
> When set to normal (or omitted, which defaults to normal), each iteration of the animation progresses from the 0% keyframe to the 100% keyframe.

animation-direction: reverse
> The reverse value sets each iteration to play in reverse keyframe order, always progressing from the 100% keyframe to the 0% keyframe. Reversing the animation direction also reverses the animation-timing-function. This property is described in "The animation-timing-function Property" on page 83.

animation-direction: alternate
> The alternate value means the first iteration (and each subsequent odd-numbered iteration) should proceed from 0% to 100%, and the second iteration (and each subsequent even-numbered cycle) should reverse direction, proceeding from 100% to 0%.

animation-direction: alternate-reverse
> The alternate-reverse value is similar to the alternate value, except the odd-numbered iterations are in the reverse direction, and the even-numbered animation iterations are in the normal direction. alternate-reverse alternates the direction of each iteration, beginning with reverse. The first iteration (and each subsequent odd numbered iteration) proceeds from 100% to 0%; the second iteration (and each subsequent even-numbered cycle) reverses direction, going from 100% to 0%:

```
.ball {
    animation-name: bouncing;
    animation-duration: 400ms;
    animation-iteration-count: infinite;
    animation-direction: alternate-reverse;
}
@keyframes bouncing {
    from {
        transforms: translateY(500px);
    }
    to {
        transforms: translateY(0);
    }
}
```

In this example, we are bouncing our ball, but we want to start by dropping it, not by throwing it up in the air: we want it to alternate between going down and up, rather than up and down, so `animation-direction: alternate-reverse` is the most appropriate value for our needs. ▶

This is a very rudimentary way of making a ball bounce. When balls are bouncing, they are moving slowest when they reach their apex and fastest when they reach their nadir. We included this example here to illustrate the `alternate-reverse` animation directions. We'll revisit the bouncing animation again later to make it more realistic with the addition of timing (see "The `animation-timing-function` Property" on page 83). There we will also discuss how, when the animation is iterating in the reverse direction, the `animation-timing-function` is reversed.

## The `animation-delay` Property

The `animation-delay` property defines how long the browser waits after the animation is attached to the element before beginning the first animation iteration. The default value is `0s`, meaning the animation will commence immediately when it is applied. A positive value will delay the start of the animation until the prescribed time, listed as the value of the `animation-delay` property has elapsed. A negative value will cause the animation to begin immediately—but it will start partway through the animation.

The `animation-delay` property sets the time, defined in seconds (`s`) or milliseconds (`ms`), that the animation will wait between when the animation is attached to the element and when the animation begins executing. By default, the animation begins iterating as soon as it is applied to the element, with a 0-second delay.

# animation-delay

**Values:**        `<time>`

**Initial value:**  `0s`

**Applies to:**     All elements, `::before` and `::after` pseudo-elements

**Inherited:**      No

Unlike `animation-duration`, a negative value for the `animation-delay` property is valid. Negative values for `animation-delay` can create interesting effects. A negative delay will execute the animation immediately but will begin animating the element part way through the attached animation. For example, if `animation-delay: -4s` and `animation-duration: 10s` are set on an element, the animation will begin immediately but will start approximately 40% of the way through the first animation.

I say "approximately" because it will not necessarily start at the 40% keyframe block: when the 40% mark of an animation occurs depends on the value of the `animation-timing-function`. If `animation-timing-function: linear` is set, then it will be 40% through the animation, at the 40% keyframe, if there is one:

```
div {
  animation-name: move;
  animation-duration: 10s;
  animation-delay: -4s;
  animation-timing-function: linear;
}

@keyframes move {
  from {
    transform: translateX(0);
  }
  to {
    transform: translateX(1000px);
  }
}
```

In this `linear` animation example, we have a 10-second animation with a 4-second delay. In this case, the animation will start immediately 40% of the way through the animation, with the `div` translated 400 pixels to the right of its original position. ▶

---

If an animation is set to occur 10 times, with a delay of -800 milliseconds and an animation duration of 200 milliseconds, the element will start animating right away, at the beginning of the fifth iteration:

```
.ball {
  animation-name: bounce;
  animation-duration: 200ms;
  animation-delay: -600ms;
  animation-iteration-count: 10;
  animation-timing-function: ease-in;
  animation-direction: alternate;
}
@keyframes bounce {
  from {
    transform: translateY(0);
  }
  to {
    transform: translateY(500px);
  }
}
```

Instead of animating for 2,000 milliseconds (200 ms x 10 = 2,000 ms), or 2 seconds, starting in the normal direction, the ball will animate for 1,400 milliseconds with the animation starting immediately—but at the start of the fourth iteration, and in the reverse direction. The animation-direction is set to alternate, meaning every even iteration iterates in the reverse direction from the 100% keyframe to the 0% keyframe. The fourth iteration, which is an even-numbered iteration, is the first visible iteration. ▶

The animation will throw the animationstart event immediately. The animationend event will occur at the 1,400-millisecond mark. The ball will be tossed up, rather than bounced, throwing 6 animationiteration events, after 200, 400, 600, 800, 1,000, and 1,200 milliseconds. While the iteration count was set to 10, we only get 6 animationiteration events because we are only getting 7 iterations; 3 iterations didn't occur because of the negative animation-delay, and the last iteration concluded at the same time as the animationend event. Remember, when an animationiteration event would occur at the same time as an animationend event, the animationiteration event does not occur.

Let's take a deeper look at animation events before continuing.

## Animation Events

There are three different types of animation events: animationstart, animation iteration, and animationend. For browsers still prefixing animations, these events are supported when written as webkitAnimationStart, webkitAnimationIteration,

and `webkitAnimationEnd`. Each event has three read-only properties of `animation`
`Name`, `elapsedTime`, and `pseudoElement`, unprefixed in all browsers.

The `animationstart` event occurs at the start of the animation: after the `animation-`
`delay` (if present) has expired, or immediately if there is no delay set. If a negative
`animation-delay` value is present, the `animationstart` will fire immediately, with an
`elapsedTime` equal to the absolute value of the delay in supporting browsers. In
browsers where prefixing is still necessary, the `elapsedTime` is 0:

```
.noAnimationEnd {
    animation-name: myAnimation;
    animation-duration: 1s;
    animation-iteration-count: infinite;
}

.startAndEndSimultaneously {
    animation-name: myAnimation;
    animation-duration: 0s;
    animation-iteration-count: infinite;
}
```

The `animationend` event occurs when the animation finishes. If the `animation-`
`iteration-count` is set to `infinite` as long as the `animation-duration` is set to a
time greater than 0, the event will never fire. If the `animation-duration` is set or
defaults to 0 seconds, even when the iteration count is infinite `animationstart` and
`animationend` will occur virtually simultaneously, in that order.

The `animationiteration` event fires *between* iterations. The `animationend` event ▶
fires at the conclusion of iterations that do not occur at the same time as the conclusion of the animation itself; the `animationiteration` and `animationend` events do
not fire simultaneously:

```
.noAnimationIteration {
    animation-name: myAnimation;
    animation-duration: 1s;
    animation-iteration-count: 1;
}
```

In the `.noAnimationIteration` example, with the `animation-iteration-count` set
to a single occurrence, the animation ends at the conclusion of the first and only iteration. When the `animationiteration` event would occur at the same time as an
`animationend`, the `animationend` event occurs, but the `animationiteration` event
does not. The `animationiteration` does not fire unless an animation cycle ends and
another begins.

When the `animation-iteration-count` property is omitted, or when its value is 1 or
less, no `animationiteration` event will be fired. As long as an iteration finishes (even

if it's a partial iteration) and the next iteration begins, if the duration is greater than 0s, an `animationiteration` event will occur.

If the `animation-iteration-count` is omitted, or has an invalid value, it defaults to `animation-iteration-count: 1`. Because the `animationiteration` event does not fire if it would occur at the same time as the `animationend`, the `animationiteration` event will not occur when `animation-iteration-count` is omitted, even though a full cycle of the animation may occur:

```
.noAnimationIteration {
    animation-name: myAnimation;
    animation-duration: 1s;
    animation-iteration-count: 4;
    animation-delay: -3s;
}
```

When an animation iterates through fewer cycles than listed in the `animation-iteration-count` because of a negative `animation-delay`, there are no `animationiteration` events for the non-occurring cycles. In the preceding example code, there are no `animationiteration` events, as the first three cycles do not occur (due to the `-3s animation-delay`), and the last cycle finishes at the same time the animation ends. ▶

In that example, the `elapsedTime` on the `animationstart` event is 3, as it is equal to the absolute value of the delay. This is supported in browsers that can handle unprefixed animations.

### Animation chaining

You can use `animation-delay` to chain animations together so the next animation starts immediately after the conclusion of the preceding animation:

```
.rainbow {
    animation-name: red, orange, yellow, blue, green;
    animation-duration: 1s, 3s, 5s, 7s, 11s;
    animation-delay: 3s, 4s, 7s, 12s, 19s;
}
```

In this example, the `red` animation starts after a three-second delay and lasts one second, meaning the `animationend` event occurs at the four-second mark. This example starts each subsequent animation at the conclusion of the previous animation. This is known as *animation chaining*. ▶

By including a four-second delay on the second animation, the `orange` animation will begin interpolating the @keyframe property values at the four-second mark, starting the `orange` animation immediately at the conclusion of the `red` animation. The `orange` animation concludes at the seven-second mark—it lasts 3 seconds, starting after a four-second delay—which is the delay set on the third, or `yellow`, animation, making the `yellow` animation begin immediately after the `orange` animation ends.

This is an example of chaining animations on a single element. You can also use the `animation-delay` property to chain the animations for different elements:

```
li:first-of-type {
    animation-name: red;
    animation-duration: 1s;
    animation-delay: 3s;
}
li:nth-of-type(2) {
    animation-name: orange;
    animation-duration: 3s;
    animation-delay: 4s;
}
li:nth-of-type(3)  {
    animation-name: yellow;
    animation-duration: 5s;
    animation-delay: 7s;
}
li:nth-of-type(4) {
    animation-name: green;
    animation-duration: 7s;
    animation-delay: 12s;
}
li:nth-of-type(5) {
    animation-name: blue;
    animation-duration: 11s;
    animation-delay: 19s;
}
```

If you want a group of list items to animate in order, ⏵ appearing as if the animations were chained in sequence, the `animation-delay` of each list item should be the combined time of the `animation-duration` and `animation-delay` of the previous animation.

The `animation-delay` property is an appropriate method of using CSS animation properties to chain animations. There is one caveat: animations are the lowest priority on the UI thread. Therefore, if you have a script running that is occupying the user interface (or UI) thread, depending on the browser and which properties are being animated and what property values are set on the element, the browser may let the delays expire while waiting until the UI thread is available before starting the animations.

Some, but not all, animations in all browsers take place on the UI thread. In most browsers, when opacity or transforms are being animated, the animation takes place on the GPU, instead of the CPU, and doesn't rely on the UI thread's availability. If those properties are not part of the animation, the unavailability of the UI thread can lead to jank. Changing the opacity, transforming, or putting an element in 3D space puts the element in its own independent layer to be drawn by the graphics processor, using GPU instead of CPU and the potentially blocked UI thread.

```
/* Don't do this */
* {
    transform: translateZ(0);
}
```

On devices and browsers that support 3D animation, putting an element into 3D space moves that element into its own layer, allowing for jank-free animations. For this reason, the translateZ hack—the thing I just told you not to do—became overused. While putting a few elements onto their own layers with this hack is OK, some devices have limited video memory. Each independent layer you create uses video memory and takes time to move from the UI thread to the composited layer on the GPU. The more layers you create, the higher the performance cost.

Edge, Chrome, Opera, and Safari can all be optimized this way. Firefox currently can't. It's likely that additional animatable properties will be animated on the GPU on composite layers off-thread in the near future.

For improved performance, whenever possible, include transform and opacity in your animations over top, left, bottom, right, and visibility. Not only does it improve performance by using the GPU over the CPU, but when you change box-model properties, the browser needs to reflow and repaint, which is bad for performance. Just don't put everything on the GPU, or you'll find different performance issues.

In the preceding scenario in a nonperformant browser, if it took 11 seconds for the browser to download, parse, and execute the document's JavaScript, the animation delay for the first 3 list items will expire before the UI thread is able to animate the properties. In this case, the first three animations—red, orange, and yellow—will begin simultaneously when the JavaScript finishes executing, with the fourth animation—green—starting a second later, before the orange and yellow animations have finished animating. In this scenario, only the last animation—blue—would start as designed: when the previous animation ended.

For this reason, you may want to attach animations to elements based on an ancestor class that gets added when the document is ready, with JavaScript.

If you are able to rely on JavaScript, another way of chaining animations is listening for animationend events to start subsequent animations: ⊙

```
document.querySelectorAll('li')[0].addEventListener( 'animationend',
    function(e) {
        document.querySelectorAll('li')[1].style.animationName = 'orange';
    },
    false );

document.querySelectorAll('li')[1].addEventListener( 'animationend',
    function(e) {
        document.querySelectorAll('li')[2].style.animationName = 'yellow';
    },
    false );

document.querySelectorAll('li')[2].addEventListener( 'animationend',
    function(e) {
        document.querySelectorAll('li')[3].style.animationName = 'green';
    },
    false );

document.querySelectorAll('li')[3].addEventListener( 'animationend',
    function(e) {
        document.querySelectorAll('li')[4].style.animationName = 'blue';
    },
    false );

li:first-of-type {
  animation-name: red;
  animation-duration: 1s;
}
li:nth-of-type(2) {
  animation-duration: 3s;
}
li:nth-of-type(3)  {
  animation-duration: 5s;
}
li:nth-of-type(4) {
  animation-duration: 7s;
}
li:nth-of-type(5)  {
  animation-duration: 11s;
}
```

In this example, there is an event handler on each of the first four list items listening for that list item's animationend event. When the animationend event occurs, the event listeners add an animation-name to the subsequent list item.

This animation chaining method doesn't employ `animation-delay`. Instead of using this CSS property, it employs JavaScript event listeners to attach animations to the element by setting the `animation-name` property when the `animationend` event is thrown.

In our CSS snippet, you'll note that the `animation-name` was only included for the first list item. The other list items only have an `animation-duration`—with no `animation-name`, and therefore no attached animations. Adding `animation-name` is what attaches and starts the animation. To start or restart an animation, the animation name or identifier must be removed and then added back—at which point all the animation properties take effect, including `animation-delay`.

Instead of writing:

```
document.querySelectorAll('li')[2].addEventListener( 'animationend',
  function(e) {
      document.querySelectorAll('li')[3].style.animationName = 'green';
  },
  false );

document.querySelectorAll('li')[3].addEventListener( 'animationend',
  function(e) {
      document.querySelectorAll('li')[4].style.animationName = 'blue';
  },
  false );

  li:nth-of-type(4) {
  animation-duration: 7s;
}
li:nth-of-type(5)  {
  animation-duration: 11s;
}
```

we could have also written:

```
document.querySelectorAll('li')[2].addEventListener( 'animationend',
  function(e) {
      document.querySelectorAll('li')[3].style.animationName = 'green';
      document.querySelectorAll('li')[4].style.animationName = 'blue';
  },
false );

li:nth-of-type(4) {
  animation-duration: 7s;
}
li:nth-of-type(5)  {
  animation-delay: 7s;
  animation-duration: 11s;
}
```

When we added the blue animation name to the fifth list item with JavaScript at the same time we added green, the delay on the fifth element took effect at that point in time and started expiring.

 While changing the values of animation properties (other than name) on the element during an animation has no effect on the animation, removing or adding an animation-name does have an impact. You can't change the animation duration from 100ms to 400ms in the middle of an animation. You can't switch the delay from -200ms to 5s once the delay has already been applied. You can, however, stop and start the animation by removing it and reapplying it. In this JavaScript example, we started the animations by applying them to the elements.

In addition, setting display: none on an element terminates the animation. Updating the display back to a visible value restarts the animation from the beginning. If there is a positive value for animation-delay, the delay will have to expire before the animationstart event happens and any animations occur. If the delay is negative, the animation will start midway through an iteration, exactly as it would have if the animation had been applied any other way.

### Animation iteration delay

While there is no such property as an animation-iteration-delay, you can employ the animation-delay property, incorporate delays within your keyframe declaration, or use JavaScript to fake it. The best method for faking it depends on the number of iterations, performance, and whether the delays are all equal in length.

What is an animation iteration delay? Sometimes you want an animation to occur multiple times, but want to wait a specific amount of time between each iteration.

Let's say you want your element to grow three times, but want to wait four seconds between each one-second iteration. You can include the delay within your keyframe definition and iterate through it three times:

```
.animate3times {
    background-color: red;
    animation: color_and_scale_after_delay;
    animation-iteration-count: 3;
    animation-duration: 5s;
}

@keyframes color_and_scale_after_delay {
    80% {
        transform: scale(1);
        background-color: red;
```

```
    }
    80.1% {
        background-color: green;
        transform: scale(0.5);
    }
    100% {
        background-color: yellow;
        transform: scale(1.5);
    }
}
```

Note the first keyframe selector is at the 80% mark and matches the default state. ⊙
This will animate your element three times: it stays in the default state for 80% of the
five-second animation (or four seconds) and then moves from green to yellow and
small to big over the last one second of the animation before iterating again, stopping
after three iterations.

This method works for any number of iterations of the animation. Unfortunately, it is
only a good solution if the delay between each iteration is identical and you don't
want to reuse the animation with any other timing, such as a delay of six seconds. ⊙
If you want to change the delay between each iteration while not changing the duration of the change in size and color, you have to write a new @keyframes definition.

To enable different iteration delays between animations, we could create a single animation and bake in the effect of three different delays:

```
.animate3times {
    background-color: red;
    animation: color_and_scale_3_times;
    animation-iteration-count: 1;
    animation-duration: 15s;
}

@keyframes color_and_scale_3_times {
  0%, 13.32%, 20.01%, 40%, 46.67%, 93.32% {
        transform: scale(1);
        background-color: red;
  }
    13.33%, 40.01%, 93.33% {
        background-color: green;
        transform: scale(0.5);
  }
    20%, 46.66%, 100% {
        background-color: yellow;
        transform: scale(1.5);
  }
}
```

This method may be more difficult to code and maintain. ⊙ It works for a single
cycle of the animation. To change the number of animations or the iteration delay
durations, another @keyframes declaration would be required. This example is even

less robust than the previous one, but it does allow for different between-iteration delays.

There's a solution that currently works in most browsers that is not specifically allowed in the animation specification, but it isn't disallowed—it's not currently supported in Edge, but hopefully it will be. The solution is to declare an animation multiple times, each with a different `animation-delay` value: ▶

```
.animate3times {
  animation: color_and_scale, color_and_scale, color_and_scale;
  animation-delay: 0, 4s, 10s;
  animation-duration: 1s;
}

@keyframes color_and_scale {
    0% {
        background-color: green;
        transform: scale(0.5);
    }
    100% {
        background-color: yellow;
        transform: scale(1.5);
    }
}
```

We've attached the animation three times, each with a different delay. In this case, each animation iteration concludes before the next one proceeds.

If animations overlap while they're concurrently animating, the values will be the values from the last declared animation. As is true whenever there are multiple animations changing an element's property at the same time, the animation that occurs last in the sequence of animation names will override any animations occurring before it in the list of names. In declaring three `color_and_scale` animations but at different intervals, the value of the property of the last iteration of the `color_and_scale` animation will override the values of the previous ones that haven't yet concluded. ▶

The safest, most robust and most cross-browser-friendly method of faking an `animation-iteration-delay` property is to use animation events. On `animationend`, detach the animation from the element, then reattach it after the iteration delay. If all the iteration delays are the same, you can use `setInterval`; if they vary, use `setTimeout`:

```
var iteration = 0;
var el = document.getElementById('myElement');

el.addEventListener('animationend', function(e) {
  var time = ++iteration * 1000;

  el.classList.remove('animationClass');
```

```
    setTimeout(function() {
      el.classList.add('animationClass');
    }, time);

  });
```

This example animates `myElement` infinitely, adding an additional second between each iteration of the animation. ▶

# The `animation-timing-function` Property

Similar to the `transition-timing-function` property, the `animation-timing-function` property describes how the animation will progress over one cycle of its duration, or iteration.

---

### animation-timing-function

| | |
|---|---|
| **Values:** | `ease` \| `linear` \| `ease-in` \| `ease-out` \| `ease-in-out` \| `step-start` \| `step-end` \| `steps(<integer>, start)` \| `steps(<integer>, end)` \| `cubic-bezier(<number>, <number>, <number>, <number>)` |
| **Initial value:** | `ease` |
| **Applies to:** | All elements, `::before` and `::after` pseudo-elements |
| **Inherited:** | No |

---

Other than the step timing functions, described in "The step timing functions" on page 86, the timing functions are all Bézier curves. Just like the `transition-timing-function`, the CSS specification provides for five predefined Bézier curve keyterms, as shown in Figure 3-1 and Table 3-1.

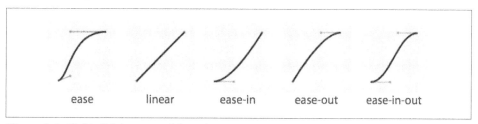

*Figure 3-1. Cubic Bézier named functions*

*Table 3-1. Bézier curve keyterms*

| Timing function | Cubic Bézier value |
|---|---|
| ease | cubic-bezier(0.25, 0.1, 0.25, 1) |
| linear | cubic-bezier(0, 0, 1, 1) |
| ease-in | cubic-bezier(0.42, 0, 1, 1) |
| ease-out | cubic-bezier(0, 0, 0.58, 1) |
| ease-in-out | cubic-bezier(0.42, 0, 0.58, 1) |

A handy tool to visualize Bézier curves and to create your own is Lea Verou's cubic Bézier visualizer (*http://cubic-bezier.com*).

The default ease is equal to cubic-bezier(0.25, 0.1, 0.25, 1), which has a slow start, then speeds up, and ends slowly. This function is similar to ease-in-out at cubic-bezier(0.42, 0, 0.58, 1), which has a greater acceleration at the beginning. linear is equal to cubic-bezier(0, 0, 1, 1), and, as the name describes, creates an animation that animates at a constant speed.

ease-in is equal to cubic-bezier(0.42, 0, 1, 1), which creates an animation that is slow to start, gains speed, then stops abruptly. The opposite ease-out timing function is equal to cubic-bezier(0, 0, 0.58, 1), starting at full speed, then slowing progressively as it reaches the conclusion of the animation iteration.

If none of these work for you, you can create your own Bézier curve timing function by passing four values, such as:

```
animation-timing-function: cubic-bezier(0.2, 0.4, 0.6, 0.8);
```

Bézier curves are mathematically defined parametric curves used in two-dimensional graphic applications. See Table 2-3 for examples of curves you can define yourself in CSS.

The Bézier curve takes four values, defining the originating position of the two handles. In CSS, the anchors are at 0, 0 and 1, 1. The first two values define the x and y of the first point or handle of the curve, and the last two are the x and y of the second handle of the curve. The x values must be between 0 and 1, or the Bézier curve is invalid. When creating your own Bézier curve, remember: the steeper the curve, the faster the motion. The flatter the curve, the slower the motion.

While the x values must be between 0 and 1, by using values for y that are greater than 1 or less than 0, you can create a bouncing effect, making the animation bounce up and down between values, rather than going consistently in a single direction:

```
.snake {
  animation-name: shrink;
  animation-duration: 10s;
  animation-timing-function: cubic-bezier(0, 4, 1, -4);
  animation-fill-mode: both;
}

@keyframes shrink {
  0% {
    width: 500px;
  }
  100% {
    width: 100px;
  }
}
```

This `animation-timing-function` value makes the property values go outside the boundaries of the values set in the 0% and 100% keyframes. In this example, we are shrinking an element from 500px to 100px. However, because of the `cubic-bezier` values, the element we're shrinking will actually grow to be wider than the 500px width defined in the 0% keyframe and narrower than the 100px width defined in the 100% keyframe, as shown in Figure 3-2.

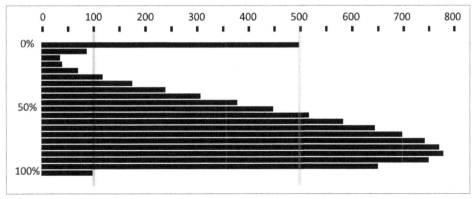

*Figure 3-2. Effect of outlandish Bézier curve*

In this scenario, with `animation-timing-function: cubic-bezier(0, 4, 1, -4);` set on an animation that is shrinking an element from from 500px to 100px wide, the snake starts with a width of 500px, defined in the 0% keyframe. It then quickly shrinks down to a width of about 40px, which is narrower than `width: 100px;` (which was declared in the 100% keyframe) before slowly expanding to about 750px wide, which is larger than the original width of `width: 500px` declared as the original (and widest) declared width. It then quickly shrinks back down to `width: 100px`, which is the value defined in the 100% keyframe. You can test this and your own cubic Bézier values. ⊙

You may have realized that the curve created by our animation is the same curve as our Bézier curve. Just like our s-curve goes below and above our bounding box, the width of our animation goes narrower than the smaller width we set of 100px and wider than the larger width we set of 500px.

The Bézier curve has the appearance of a snake, going up and down and up again, because one y coordinate is positive and the other negative. If both are positive values greater than 1 or both are negative values less than -1, the Bézier curve is arc-shaped, going above or below one of the values set, but not bouncing out of bounds on both ends like the s-curve above.

The timing function declared for the `animation-timing-function` is the timing for the normal animation direction, when the animation is progressing from the 0% mark to the 100% mark. When the animation is running in the reverse direction, from the 100% mark to the 0% mark, the animation timing function is reversed:

```
.ball {
  animation-name: bounce;
  animation-duration: 1s;
  animation-iteration-count: infinite;
  animation-timing-function: ease-in;
  animation-direction: alternate;
}

@keyframes bounce {
  0% {
    transform: translateY(0);
  }
  100% {
    transform: translateY(500px);
  }
}
```

If we remember the bouncing ball example ▶, when the ball is dropping it gets faster as it nears its nadir at the 100% keyframe, with the `animation-timing-function` set to `ease-in`. When it is bouncing up, it is animating in the reverse direction, from 100% to 0%, so the `animating-timing-function` is reversed as well, to `ease-out`, slowing down as it reaches its apex. Our original defaulted to `ease`. This timing function makes the bouncing ball look a bit more realistic.

## The step timing functions

The step timing functions, `step-start`, `step-end`, and `steps()`, aren't Bézier curves. Rather, they're *tweening* definitions.

The `steps()` timing function divides the animation into a series of equal-length steps. `steps()` takes two parameters: the number of steps and the direction.

The steps() function is most useful when it comes to character or sprite animation. If you want to animate complex shapes that subtly change, like the drawings or pictures in a flip book, the steps() timing function is the solution.

The number of steps is the first parameter; its value must be a positive integer. The animation will be divided equally into the number of steps provided. For example, if the animation duration is 1 second and the number of steps is 5, the animation will be divided into five 200-millisecond steps, with the element being redrawn to the page 5 times, at 200-millisecond intervals, moving 20% through the animation at each interval.

If an animation were to pass through 5 steps, that means it either draws the animation at the 0%, 20%, 40%, 60%, and 80% keyframes or at the 20%, 40%, 60%, 80%, and 100% keyframes. It will either skip drawing the 100% or the 0% keyframe. That is where the *direction* parameter comes in.

The *direction* parameter takes one of two values: either start or end. The direction determines if the function is left- or right-continuous: basically, if the 0% or the 100% keyframe is going to be skipped. Including start as the second parameter will create a left-continuous function, meaning the first step happens when the animation begins, skipping the 0%, but including the 100%. Including end or omitting the second parameter (end is the default direction) will create a right-continuous function. This mean the first step will be at the 0% mark, and the last step will be before the 100% mark. With end, the 100% keyframe will not be seen unless animation-fill-mode of either forwards or both is set. See "The animation-fill-mode Property" on page 95.

The direction parameter can be hard to remember. I like to think of it this way: the *start* value *skips* the start value of 0%, and the *end* value *skips* the ending value of the 100% keyframe.

The step-start value is equal to steps(1, start), with only a single step displaying the 100% keyframe. The step-end value is equal to steps(1, end), which displays only the 0% keyframe.

Consider the flip book. A flip book is a book with a series of pictures. Each page contains a single drawing or picture that changes slightly from one page to the next, like one frame from a movie reel or cartoon stamped onto each page. When the pages of a flip book are flipped through rapidly (hence the name), the pictures appear as an animated motion. You can create similar animations with CSS using an image sprite, the background-position property, and the steps() timing function.

Figure 3-3 shows an image sprite containing several images that change just slightly, like the drawings on the individual pages of our flip book.

*Figure 3-3. Sprite of dancing*

We put all of our slightly differing images into a single image called a *sprite*. Each image in our sprite is a frame in the single animated image we're creating.

We create a container element that is the size of a single image of our sprite and attach the sprite as the container element's background image. We then animate the `background-position`, using the `steps()` timing function so we only see a single instance of the changing image of our sprite at a time. The number of steps in our `steps()` timing function is the number of occurrences of the image in our sprite. The number of steps defines how many stops our background image makes to complete a single animation.

The sprite in Figure 3-3 has 22 images, each 56 x 100 pixels. The total size of our sprite is 1232 x 100 pixels. We set our container to the individual image size: 56 x 100 pixels. We set our sprite as our background image: the initial or default value of `background-position` is `top left`, which is the same as `0 0`. Our image will appear at `0 0`, which is a good default: older browsers that don't support CSS animation will simply display the first image from our sprite:

```
.dancer {
  height: 100px;
  width: 56px;
  background-image: url(../images/dancer.png);
  ....
}
```

The trick is to use `steps()` to change the `background-position` value so that each frame is a view of a separate image within the sprite. Instead of sliding in the background image from the left, the `steps()` timing function will pop in the background image in the number of steps we declared.

We declare our animation to simply be a change in the left-right value of the `background-position`. The image is 1,232 pixels wide, so we move the background image from `0 0`, which is the left top, to `0 -1232px`, putting the sprite fully outside of our 56 x 100 pixel <div> viewport.

The values of `-1232px 0` will move the image completely to the left, outside of our containing block viewport. It will no longer show up as a background image in our 100 x 56 pixel `div` at the 100% mark unless `background-repeat` is set to repeat along the x-axis. We don't want that to happen!

With the `steps(n, end)` syntax, the 100% keyframe never gets shown as the animation runs. Had we used `start` instead of `end`, the 0% keyframe wouldn't show. With `end`, the 100% keyframe is skipped instead. Because we used `end`, the 100% keyframe—when the background image is outside of the border box of our element—doesn't show. This is what we want:

```
@keyframes dance_in_place {
  from {
      background-position: 0 0;
  }
  to {
      background-position: -1232px 0;
  }
}

.dancer {
  ....
  background-image: url(../images/dancer.png);
  animation-name: dance_in_place;
  animation-duration: 4s;
  animation-timing-function: steps(22, end);
  animation-iteration-count: infinite;
}
```

We used `steps(22, end)`. We use the `end` direction to show the 0% keyframe, but not the 100% keyframe. What may have seemed like a complex animation is very simple: just like a flip book, we see one frame of the sprite at a time. Our keyframe animation simply moves the background. ▶

### Adding a second animation

Our dancer is dancing in place. Most dancers move around when they dance. We can add a little left-and-right and back-and-forth motion by adding a second animation:

```
@keyframes move_around {
  0%, 100% {
    transform: translate(0, -40px) scale(0.9);
  }
  25%  {
    transform: translate(40px, 0)  scale(1);
  }
  50%  {
    transform: translate(0, 40px)  scale(1.1);
  }
  75%  {
    transform: translate(-40px, 0) scale(1);
  }
}
```

We create a second keyframe animation called move_around and attach it to our dancer element as a second animation with comma-separated animation property declarations: ▶

```
.dancer {
    ....
    background-image: url(../images/dancer.png);
    animation-name: dance_in_place, move_around;
    animation-duration: 4s, 16s;
    animation-timing-function: steps(22, end), steps(5, end);
    animation-iteration-count: infinite;
}
```

Note that each animation property has two comma-separated values except animation-iteration-count. If you recall, if an animation property doesn't have enough comma-separated values to match the number of animations declared by the animation-name property, the values present will be repeated until there are enough. We want both animations to continue indefinitely. As the value of infinite is for all the attached animations, we only need a single value for that property. The browser will repeat the list of animation-iteration-count values—in this case, just the single value of infinite—until it has matched an animation-iteration-count value for each animation declared.

## Animating the animation-timing-function

The animation-timing-function is not an animatable property, but it can be included in a keyframe to alter the current timing of the animation.

When included within a keyframe, the animation-timing-function doesn't transition from one value to another over time. Rather, the timing function applies between keyframes, updating the timing function when it reaches a keyframe that has a timing function defined.

While none of the animation properties are animatable, animation-timing-function is the only CSS animation property that has an effect when specified on individual keyframes. Unlike animatable properties, the animation-timing-function values aren't interpolated over time. When included in a keyframe within the @keyframes definition, the timing function for the properties declared within that same keyframe will change to the new animation-timing-function value when that keyframe is reached, as shown in Figure 3-4:

```
@keyframes width {
  0% {
    width: 200px;
    animation-timing-function: linear;
  }
  50% {
    width: 350px;
```

```
    animation-timing-function: ease-in;
  }
  100% {
    width: 500px;
  }
}
```

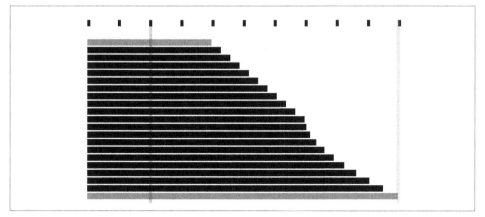

*Figure 3-4. Animation timing function can be changed midanimation*

In other words, the rate at which the animation proceeds can be altered mid anima‐
tion. In the preceding example, as shown in Figure 3-4, halfway through the anima‐
tion, we switch from a linear animation progression for the `width` property to one
that eases in. ⓟ

We can include the `animation-timing-function` within our keyframe animation
definitions to override this default inverting behavior or to control the timing in any
other way we please. The `animation-timing-function` property isn't animated in the
sense of changing from one value to another over time. Rather, it changes from
one value to the next when it reaches a keyframe selector that declares a change to
that value.

Specifying the `animation-timing-function` within the `to` or `100%` keyframe will have
no effect on the animation. When included in the `from` or `0%` keyframe, the animation
will follow the `animation-timing-function` specified in the keyframe definition,
overriding the element's default or declared `animation-timing-function`.

> The specification states explicitly the timing function should only
> impact the progression of an animation if it is declared in any key‐
> frame other than the `to` or `100%` keyframe values. An `animation-
> timing-function` declaration in the `100%` or `to` keyframe has no
> effect, as per current implementations and the specification.

If the `animation-timing-function` property is included in a keyframe, only the properties also included in that keyframe block will have their timing function impacted. This is not currently specified in the CSS specification, but it is implemented as such and is expected to be included in the final specification. If we take our W animation as an example:

```
@keyframes W {
    from {
      left: 0;
      top: 0;
    }
    25%, 75% {
      top: 100%;
    }
    50% {
      top: 50%;
    }
    to {
      left: 100%;
      top: 0;
    }
}
```

This follows the idea that conceptually, when an animation is set on an element or pseudo-element, it is as if a set of keyframes is created for each property that is present in any of the keyframes, as if an animation is run independently for each property that is being animated. It's as if the W animation were made up of two animations that run simultaneously: `W_part1` and `W_part2`.

```
@keyframes W_part1 {
    from, to {
      top: 0;
    }
    25%, 75% {
      top: 100%;
    }
    50% {
      top: 50%;
    }
}

@keyframes W_part2 {
    from {
      left: 0;
    }
    to {
      left: 100%;
    }
}
```

The `animation-timing-function` that is set on any of the keyframes is added to the progression of only the properties that are defined at that keyframe:

```
@keyframes W {
    from {
      left: 0;
      top: 0;
    }
    25%, 75% {
      top: 100%;
    }
    50% {
      animation-timing-function: ease-in;
      top: 50%;
    }
    to {
      left: 100%;
      top: 0;
    }
}
```

You can have multiple occurrences of a keyframe value, such as 50%, as the current implementation stands, but the `animation-timing-function` and property have to be in the same selector block for the `animation-timing-function` change to have an impact. The preceding code will change the `animation-timing-function` to `ease-in` for the `top` property only, not the `left` property, impacting only the `W_part1` section of our `W` animation.

However, with the following animation, the `animation-timing-function` (in a keyframe block that has no property/value declarations) will have no effect:

```
@keyframes W {
    from {
      left: 0;
      top: 0;
    }
    25%, 75% {
      top: 100%;
    }
    50% {
      animation-timing-function: ease-in;
    }
    50% {
      top: 50%;
    }
    to {
      left: 100%;
      top: 0;
    }
}
```

How is it useful to change the timing function midanimation? In the bounce animation, we had a frictionless environment: the ball bounced forever, never losing momentum. We had a very simple animation that iterated forever. The `ease-in` timing function made it speed up as it dropped, when it was in the `normal` animation direction. We took advantage of timing functions being inverted in the reverse animation direction: in this case, as if it was set to `ease-out` in the reverse direction. With our infinite animation, the ball sped up as it dropped and slowed as it rose because the timing function was inverted from `ease-in` to `ease-out` by default as the animation proceeded from the normal to reverse direction every other iteration.

In reality, friction exists; momentum is lost. Balls will not continue to bounce indefinitely. If we want our bouncing ball to look natural, we have to make it bounce less high as it loses energy with each impact. To do this, we need a single animation that bounces multiple times, losing momentum on each bounce, while switching between `ease-in` and `ease-out` at each apex and nadir:

```
@keyframes bounce {
  0% {
    transform: translateY(0);
    animation-timing-function: ease-in;
  }
  30% {
    transform: translateY(100px);
    animation-timing-function: ease-in;
  }
  58% {
    transform: translateY(200px);
    animation-timing-function: ease-in;
  }
  80% {
    transform: translateY(300px);
    animation-timing-function: ease-in;
  }
  95% {
    transform: translateY(360px);
    animation-timing-function: ease-in;
  }
  15%, 45%, 71%, 89%, 100% {
    transform: translateY(380px);
    animation-timing-function: ease-out;
  }
}
```

This animation loses height after a few bounces, eventually stopping. ⏵ This more realistic animation has a single iteration, with the granular control provided via the keyframe blocks.

In the case of a single iteration, we can't rely on the `animation-direction` to change our timing function. We need to ensure that while each bounce causes the ball to lose momentum, it still speeds up with gravity and slows down as it reaches its apex. Because we will have only a single iteration, we control the timing by including animation-timing-function within our keyframes. At every apex, we switch to ease-in, and at every nadir, or bounce, we switch to ease-out.

## The animation-play-state property

The animation-play-state property defines whether the animation is running or paused.

<table>
<tr><td colspan="2" align="center">**animation-play-state**</td></tr>
<tr><td>**Values:**</td><td>running | paused</td></tr>
<tr><td>**Initial value:**</td><td>running</td></tr>
<tr><td>**Applies to:**</td><td>All elements, ::before and ::after pseudo-elements</td></tr>
<tr><td>**Inherited:**</td><td>No</td></tr>
</table>

When set to the default running, the animation proceeds as normal. If set to paused, the animation will be paused. When paused, the animation is still applied to the element, halted at the progress it had made before being paused. When set back to running or returned to the default of running, it restarts from where it left off, as if the "clock" that controls the animation had stopped and started again.

If the property is set to animation-play-state: paused during the delay phase of the animation, the delay clock is also paused and resumes expiring as soon as animation-play-state is set back to running. ⊙

## The animation-fill-mode Property

The animation-fill-mode property defines what values are applied by the animation before and after the animation iterations are executed. The animation-fill-mode property enables us to define whether or not an element's property values are applied by the animation outside of the animation execution. The duration of the animation execution is set by the number of iterations multiplied by the duration, less the absolute value of any negative delay.

With animation-fill-mode, we can define how the animation impacts the element on which it is set before the animationstart and after the animationend events are fired. We can define whether the property values set in the 0% keyframe are applied to the element during the expiration of any animation delay, and if the property values that exist when the animationend event is fired continue to be applied to the animated element after the animation's conclusion, or if the properties revert to the values they had in their initial state prior to the attachment of the animation.

By default, an animation will not affect the property values of the element immediately if there is a positive animation-delay applied. Rather, animation property values are applied when the animation-delay expires, when the animationstart event is fired. By default, the animation property values are applied until the last iteration has completed: at the completion of the animation, when the animationend event is fired. At that time, the element's property values revert back to its nonanimated values.

The animation-fill-mode property lets us apply the property values of any from or 0% keyframes to an element from the time the animation is applied to that element until the expiration of the animation delay. It also enables us to maintain the property values of the 100% or to keyframe after the last animation cycle is complete, from the time the animationend event has fired until forever—or until the animation is removed from the element.

---

## animation-fill-mode

**Values:**       none | forwards | backwards | both

**Initial value:**  none

**Applies to:**   All elements, ::before and ::after pseudo-elements

**Inherited:**    No

---

The default value is none, which means the animation has no effect when it is not executing: the animation's 0% keyframe block property values are not applied to the animated element until the animation-delay has expired, when the animationstart event is fired.

When the value is set to backwards, the property values from the 0% or from keyframe (if there is one) will be applied to the element as soon as the animation is applied to the element. The 0% keyframe property values are applied immediately (or 100% keyframe, if the value of the animation-direction property is reversed or reversed-alternate), without waiting for the `animation-delay` time to expire, before the `animationstart` event fires.

The value of `forwards` means when the animation is done executing—has concluded the last part of the last iteration as defined by the `animation-iteration-count` value —it continues to apply the values of the properties at the values as they were when the `animationend` event occurred. If the `iteration-count` has an integer value, this will be either the 100% keyframe, or, if the last iteration was in the reverse direction, the 0% keyframe.

The value of `both` applies both the `backwards` effect of applying the property values when the animation is attached to the element and the `forwards` value of persisting the property values from when the `animationend` event occurred.

If the `animation-iteration-count` is a float value, and not an integer, the last iteration will not end on the 0% or 100% keyframe: the animation will end its execution partway through an animation cycle. If the `animation-fill-mode` was set `forwards` or `both`, the element will maintain the property values it had when the `animationend` event occurred. For example, if the `animation-iteration-count` is `6.5`, and the `animation-timing-function` is linear, the `animationend` event fires and the values of the properties at the 50% mark (whether or not a 50% keyframe is explicitly declared) will stick, as if the `animation-play-state` had been set to `pause` at that point.

For example, if we take the following code:

```
@keyframes move_me {
  0% {
    transform: translateX(0);
  }
  100% {
    transform: translateX(1000px);
  }
}

.moved {
  animation-name: move_me;
  animation-duration: 10s;
  animation-timing-function: linear;
  animation-iteration-count: 0.6;
  animation-fill-mode: forwards;
}
```

The animation will only go through 0.6 iterations. Being a linear 10-second animation, it will stop at the 60% mark 6 seconds into the animation, when the element is translated 600 pixels to the right. With `animation-fill-mode` set to `forwards` or `both`, the animation will stop animating when it is translated 600 pixels to the right, holding the moved element 600 pixels to the right of its original position, keeping it translated indefinitely, or until the animation is detached from the element.

In Safari 9 and earlier, forwards and both will set the values from the 100% keyframe onto the element, no matter the direction of the last iteration or whether the animation otherwise ended on the 100% keyframe or elsewhere in the animation. ⊙ In the preceding example, in Safari 9, the .moved element will jump from being translated by 400 pixels to the right to be 1,000 pixels to the right of where it normally would have been and stay there indefinitely or until the animation is detached from the moved element. In Safari 9 and earlier, it doesn't matter whether the last iteration was normal or reverse, or whether the animation ended 25% or 75% of the way through an animation cycle; animation-fill-mode: forwards; causes the animation to jump to the 100% frame and stay there. This follows an older version of the specification, but we expect it will be updated to match the updated specification and all other evergreen browsers.

The backwards value controls what happens to the element from the time the animation is attached to the element until the time the animation delay expires, the animation starts executing, and the animationstart event is fired. Before the animation starts executing (during the period specified by a positive animation-delay value), the animation applies the values it will have when the animation starts executing. If the animation-direction is normal or alternate, the values specified in the animation's 0% keyframe are applied immediately when the animation is attached. If the animation-direction is reverse or alternate-reverse, the property values of the 100% keyframe are used.

The value of both simply means that both the forwards and backwards fill modes will be applied. Most times when you set an animation, you will set the animation-fill-mode property to both. This ensures that the animated element's properties don't jump from the element's default state to the animated state at the start of execution, and that the element's properties don't jump back to its original property values at the animation's end. Having properties jump from one value to another before or after a smooth animation is generally the opposite of what you're trying to do.

With both, as soon as the animation is attached to an element, that element will assume the properties provided in the 0% keyframe (or 100% keyframe if animation-direction is set to reverse or alternate-reverse). When the last iteration concludes, it will be as if the animation-fill-mode were set to forwards: if it was a full iteration in the normal direction, the property values of the 100% keyframe will be applied. If the last cycle was in the reverse direction, the property values of the 0% keyframe will be applied. With forwards and both, whether or not the last iteration was a full iteration, the values that were present when the animationend event occurred will stay in effect. ⊙

If the animation-duration is set to 0s and backward or both is set, the animation will stay on the 0% keyframe (or 100% keyframe if animation-direction is set to reverse or reverse-alternate) until the animation delay has expired. With no duration, it will immediately jump to the 100% keyframe (or the 0% keyframe ⊙ if animation-direction is set to reverse or reverse-alternate). If both or forwards is set, it will stay on that final keyframe in perpetuity or until the animation is removed from the element or generated content. This happens no matter the value of the animation-iteration-count, even if the count is 0. In that case, the animation start and animationend events will occur in succession at the expiration of the delay, and there will be no animationiteration event.

If the 0% or 100% keyframes are not explicitly defined, the browser uses the implied values for those keyframes: the values set forth on the element itself. If an keyframe animation has neither a 0% or 100% keyframe set, setting animation-fill-mode: backwards will have no impact. Similarly, in the case where the animation-iteration-count is an integer and no 0% or 100% keyframe is set, setting animation-fill-mode to forwards or both has no impact. If the iteration count is a float, even if there are no to or from keyframes, if there is an intermediary keyframe block with property values set, forwards, backwards, and both should have an impact, other than in Safari ≤9.

## The animation Shorthand Property

The animation shorthand property enables us to use one line instead of eight to define all the animation properties on an element. The animation property value is a list of space-separated values for the various longhand animation properties. If you are setting multiple animations on an element or pseudo-element, include the multiple space-separated animation shorthands as a comma-separated list of animations.

---

### animation

| | |
|---|---|
| **Values:** | none | <series of individual animation properties> <animation-duration> ‖ <animation-timing-function> ‖ <animation-delay> ‖ <animation-iteration-count> ‖ <animation-direction> ‖ <animation-fill-mode> ‖ <animation-play-state> ‖ <animation-name> |
| **Initial value:** | 0s ease 0s 1 normal none running none |
| **Applies to:** | All elements, ::before and ::after pseudo-elements |
| **Inherited:** | No |

---

The animation shorthand takes as its value all the other preceding animation properties, including animation-duration, animation-timing-function, animation-delay, animation-iteration-count, animation-direction, animation-fill-mode, animation-play-state, and animation-name:

```
#animated {
    animation: 200ms ease-in 50ms 1 normal running forwards slidedown;
}
```

is the equivalent of:

```
#animated {
    animation-name: slidedown;
    animation-duration: 200ms;
    animation-timing-function: ease-in;
    animation-delay: 50ms;
    animation-iteration-count: 1;
    animation-fill-mode: forwards;
    animation-direction: normal;
    animation-play-state: running;
}
```

or:

```
#animated {
    animation: 200ms ease-in 50ms forwards slidedown;
}
```

We didn't have to declare all of the values in the animation shorthand; any values that aren't declared are set to the default or initial values. The first shorthand line was long and three of the properties were set to default, so were not necessary.

It's important to remember that if you don't declare all eight values in your shorthand declaration, the ones you don't declare will get the initial value for that property. The initial or default values are:

```
animation-name: none;
animation-duration: 0s;
animation-timing-function: ease;
animation-delay: 0;
animation-iteration-count: 1;
animation-fill-mode: none;
animation-direction: normal;
animation-play-state: running;
```

The order of the shorthand is partially important. For example, there are two time properties: the first is always the duration. The second, if present, is interpreted as the delay.

While the order of all properties that make up a shorthand are important, the order of numeric values with the same unit type are always important, no matter the property. For example, in the flex shorthand, the first unitless number is the flex-grow value; the second is the `flex-shrink` factor. Similarly, for the `animation` shorthand, the first time value is always the `animation-duration`. The second, if present, is always the `animation-delay`.

The placement of the `animation-name` can also be important. If you use an animation property value as your animation identifier (which you shouldn't), the `animation-name` should be placed as the *last* property value in the `animation` shorthand. The first occurrence of a keyword that is a valid value for any of the other animation properties, such as `ease` or `running`, will be assumed to be part of the shorthand of the animation property the keyword is associated with rather than the `animation-name`. Note that `none` is basically the only word that is not a valid animation name:

```
#failedAnimation {
    animation: paused 2s;
}
```

This is the equivalent to:

```
#failedAnimation {
    animation-name: none;
    animation-duration: 2s;
    animation-delay: 0;
    animation-timing-function: ease;
    animation-iteration-count: 1;
    animation-fill-mode: none;
    animation-direction: normal;
    animation-play-state: paused;
}
```

`paused` is a valid animation name. While it may seem that the animation named `paused` with a duration of `2s` is being attached to the element, that is not what is happening. Because words within the shorthand animation are first checked against possible valid values of all animation properties other than `animation-name` first, `paused` is being set as the value of the `animation-play-state` property.

```
#anotherFailedAnimation {
    animation: running 2s ease-in-out forwards;
}
```

The preceding code snippet is the equivalent to:

```
#anotherFailedAnimation {
    animation-name: none;
    animation-duration: 2s;
    animation-delay: 0s;
    animation-timing-function: ease-in-out;
    animation-iteration-count: 1;
    animation-fill-mode: forwards;
    animation-direction: normal;
    animation-play-state: running;
}
```

The developer probably has a keyframe animation called `running`. The browser, however, sees the term and assigns it to the `animation-play-state` property rather than the `animation-name` property. With no `animation-name` declared, there is no animation attached to the element.

In light of this, `animation: 2s 3s 4s;` may seem valid, as if the following were being set:

```
#invalidName {
    animation-name: 4s;
    animation-duration: 2s;
    animation-delay: 3s;
}
```

But as we remember from "Setting Up Your Keyframe Animation" on page 57, `4s` is *not* a valid identifier. Identifiers cannot start with a digit unless escaped. For this animation to be valid, it would have to be written as `animation: 2s 3s \34 s;`

To attach multiple animations to a single element or pseudo-element, comma-separate the animation declarations:

```
.snowflake {
    animation: 3s ease-in 200ms 32 forwards falling,
               1.5s linear 200ms 64 spinning;
}
```

Our snowflake will fall while spinning for 96 seconds, spinning twice during each 3-second fall. ▶ At the end of the last animation cycle, the snowflake will stay fixed on the 100% keyframe of the `falling` @keyframes animation. We declared six of the eight animation properties for the `falling` animation and five for the spinning animation, separating the two animations with a comma.

While you'll most often see the animation name as the first value—it's easier to read that way, because of the issue with animation property keywords being valid keyframe identifiers—it is not a best practice. That is why we put the animation name at the end.

It is fine, even a good idea, to use the `animation` shorthand. Just remember that the placement of the duration, delay, and name within that shorthand are important, and omitted values will be set to their default values. Also, it is a good idea to not use any animation keyterms as your identifier.

# Animation, Specificity, and Precedence Order

In terms of specificity, the cascade, and which property values get applied to an element, animations currently supersede all other values in the cascade. When an animation is attached to an element, it takes precedence, as if the specificity was even stronger than if the keyframe animation's property values were set inline with an !important: as if <div style="keyframe-property: value !important">.

## Specificity and !important

In general, the weight of a property attached with an ID selector 1-0-0 should take precedence over a property applied by an element selector 0-0-1. However, if that property value was changed via a keyframe animation, it will be applied as if that property/value pair were added as an inline style. The current behavior in all browsers that support animation is as if the property values were declared inline with an added !important. This is wrong, according to the specifications. The animation specification states "animations override all normal rules, but are overridden by !important rules." This is a bug in the current implementations and should be resolved eventually.

A property added via a CSS animation, even if that animation was added on a CSS block with very low specificity, will be applied to the element, even if the same property is applied to the same element via a more specific selector, an inline style, or, currently, even the keyterm !important—even on three nested ID selectors. Currently, if an !important is declared on a property value within the cascade, that will not override the style that was added with an animation. ⊙ The animation is "even more !important."

That being said, don't include !important within your animation declaration block; the property/value upon which it is declared will be ignored. ⊙

## Animation Order

If there are multiple animations specifying values for the same property, the property value from the last animation applied will override the previous animations:

```
#colorchange {
  animation-name: red, green, blue;
  animation-duration: 11s, 9s, 6s;
}
```

In this code example, if red, green, and blue are all keyframe animations that change the color property to their respective names, once the animation-name and animation-duration properties are applied to #colorchange, for the first six seconds, the property values in blue will take precedence, then green for three seconds, then red for two seconds, before returning to its default property values. ⊙

The default properties of an element are not impacted before the animation starts, and the properties return to their original values after the animation ends unless an animation-fill-mode value other than the default none has been set. If animation-fill-mode: both were added to the mix, the color would always be blue, as the last animation, or blue, overrides the previous green animation, which overrides the red first animation. ⊙

## Animation Iteration and `display: none;`

If the `display` property is set to `none` on an element, any animation iterating on that element or its descendants will cease, as if the animation were detached from the element. Updating the `display` property back to a visible value will reattach all the animation properties, restarting the animation from scratch:

```
.snowflake {
    animation: spin 2s linear 5s 20;
}
```

The snowflake will spin 20 times; each spin takes 2 seconds, with the first spin starting after 5 seconds. If the snowflake element's `display` property gets set to `none` after 15 seconds, it would have completed 5 spins before disappearing (5-second delay, then 5 spins at 2 seconds each). If the snowflake `display` property changes back to anything other than `none`, the animation starts from scratch: a 5-second delay will elapse again before it starts spinning 20 times. It makes no difference how many animation cycles iterated before it disappeared from view the first time. ⊙

## Animation and the UI Thread

CSS animations have the lowest priority on the UI thread. If you attach multiple animations on page load with positive values for `animation-delay`, the delays expire as prescribed, but the animations may not begin until the UI thread is available to animate.

If the animations require the UI thread (they aren't on the GPU as described in "Animation chaining" on page 75); if you have 20 animations set with an animation delays to start animating at 1-second intervals over 20 seconds, with the `animation-delay` property on each set to 1s, 2s, 3s, 4s, and so on; if the document or application takes a long time to load, with 11 seconds between the time the animated elements were drawn to the page and the time the JavaScript finished being downloaded, parsed, and executed; the delays of the first 11 animations will have expired and will all commence when the UI thread becomes available. The remaining animations will each then begin animating at one-second intervals.

## Seizure Disorders

While you can use animations to create changing content, dynamically changing content can lead to seizures in some users. Always keep accessibility in mind, ensuring the accessibility of your website to people with epilepsy and other seizure disorders.

# Animation Events and Prefixing

Let's recap animation-related events we can access with DOM event listeners.

## animationstart

The `animationstart` event occurs at the start of the animation. If there is an `animation-delay`, this event will fire once the delay period has expired. If there is no delay, the `animationstart` event occurs when the animation is applied to the element. Even if there are no iterations, the `animationstart` event still occurs. If there are multiple animations attached to an element, an `animationstart` event will occur for each of the applied valid keyframe animations: generally, one `animationstart` for each valid `animation-name` identifier present:

```
#colorchange {
  animation: red, green, blue;
}
```

In this example, as long as the `red`, `green`, and `blue` keyframe animations are valid, while the animations will not be perceptible (as the default duration of `0s` is set on each), there will be three `animationstart` events thrown: one for each animation name.

If the browser requires the `-webkit-` prefix for the animation properties—basically, Safari 8 and earlier and Android 4.4.4 and older—the event is written as `webkitAnimationStart` instead of `animationstart`. Note the `-webkit-` prefix and the camelCasing. It is best to default to the unprefixed syntax and fall back to the prefixed version only when the unprefixed is unavailable.

## animationend

The `animationend` event occurs at the conclusion of the last animation. It only occurs once per applied animation: if an element has 3 animations applied to it, like in our `#colorchange` example, the `animationend` event will occur three times, at the end of the animation. In the example, there was no duration for any of the animations; however, the `animationend` event timing is usually equivalent to the result of the following equation:

```
(animation-duration * animation-iteration-count) + animation-delay = time
```

Even if there are no iterations, the `animationend` event still occurs once for each animation applied. If the `animation-iteration-count` is set to `infinite`, the `animationend` event never occurs.

If the browser requires the `-webkit-` prefix for the animation properties, the event is written as `webkitAnimationEnd` instead of `animationend`.

## animationiteration

The animationiteration event occurs at the end of each iteration of an animation, before the start of the next iteration. If there are no iterations, or the iteration count is less than or equal to one, the animationiteration event never occurs. If the iteration count is infinite, the animationiteration event occurs ad infinitum, unless there is no duration set or the duration is 0s.

Unlike the animationstart and animationend events, which each occur once for each animation name, the animationiteration event can occur multiple times or no times per animation name, depending on how many iterations occur. Note that the event happens between animation cycles and will not occur at the same time as an animationend event. In other words, if the animation-iteration-count is an integer, the number of animationiteration events that occur is generally one less that the value of the animation-iteration-count property as long as the absolute value of any negative delay is less than the duration.

# Other Considerations

## Printing Animations

While not actually "animating" on a printed piece of paper, when an animated element is printed, the relevant property values will be printed. Obviously, you can't see the element animating on a piece of paper, but if the animation caused an element to have a border-radius of 50%, the printed element will have a border-radius of 50%.

# About the Author

How does someone get to be the author of both *Transitions and Animations in CSS* and *Mobile HTML5* (O'Reilly), and coauthor of *CSS3 for the Real World* (SitePoint)? For **Estelle Weyl**, the journey was not a direct one. She started out as an architect, used her master's degree in health and social behavior from the Harvard School of Public Health to lead teen health programs, and then began dabbling in website development. By the time Y2K rolled around, she had become somewhat known as a web standardista at *http://www.standardista.com*.

Today, she writes a technical blog that pulls in millions of visitors, and speaks about CSS3, HTML5, JavaScript, accessibility, and mobile web development at conferences around the world. In addition to sharing esoteric programming tidbits with her reading public, Estelle has consulted for Kodak Gallery, SurveyMonkey, Visa, Samsung, Yahoo!, and Apple, among others.

When not coding, she spends her time doing construction, striving to remove the last remnants of communal hippiedom from her 1960s throwback home. Basically, it's just one more way Estelle is working to bring the world into the 21st century.

# Colophon

The animal on the cover of *Transitions and Animations in CSS* are salmon (*salmonidae*), which is a family of fish consisting of many different species. Two of the most common salmon are the Pacific salmon and the Atlantic salmon.

Pacific salmon live in the northern Pacific Ocean off the coasts of North America and Asia. There are five subspecies of Pacific salmon, with an average weight of 10 to 30 pounds. Pacific salmon are born in the fall in freshwater stream gravel beds, where they incubate through the winter and emerge as inch-long fish. They live for a year or two in streams or lakes and then head downstream to the ocean. There they live for a few years, before heading back upstream to their exact place of birth to spawn and then die.

Atlantic salmon live in the northern Atlantic Ocean off the coasts of North America and Europe. There are many subspecies of Atlantic salmon, including the trout and the char. Their average weight is 10 to 20 pounds. The Atlantic salmon family has a life cycle similar to that of its Pacific cousins, and also travels from freshwater gravel beds to the sea. A major difference between the two, however, is that the Atlantic salmon does not die after spawning; it can return to the ocean and then return to the stream to spawn again, usually two or three times.

Salmon, in general, are graceful, silver-colored fish with spots on their backs and fins. Their diet consists of plankton, insect larvae, shrimp, and smaller fish. Their unusually keen sense of smell is thought to help them navigate from the ocean back to the exact spot of their birth, upstream past many obstacles. Some species of salmon remain landlocked, living their entire lives in freshwater.

Salmon are an important part of the ecosystem, as their decaying bodies provide fertilizer for streambeds. Their numbers have been dwindling over the years, however. Factors in the declining salmon population include habitat destruction, fishing, dams that block spawning paths, acid rain, droughts, floods, and pollution.

The cover image is a 19th-century engraving from the Dover Pictorial Archive. The cover fonts are URW Typewriter and Guardian Sans. The text font is Adobe Minion Pro; the heading font is Adobe Myriad Condensed; and the code font is Dalton Maag's Ubuntu Mono.

# Get even more for your money.

## Join the O'Reilly Community, and register the O'Reilly books you own. It's free, and you'll get:

- $4.99 ebook upgrade offer
- 40% upgrade offer on O'Reilly print books
- Membership discounts on books and events
- Free lifetime updates to ebooks and videos
- Multiple ebook formats, DRM FREE
- Participation in the O'Reilly community
- Newsletters
- Account management
- 100% Satisfaction Guarantee

### Signing up is easy:

1. Go to: oreilly.com/go/register
2. Create an O'Reilly login.
3. Provide your address.
4. Register your books.

Note: English-language books only

**To order books online:**
oreilly.com/store

**For questions about products or an order:**
orders@oreilly.com

**To sign up to get topic-specific email announcements and/or news about upcoming books, conferences, special offers, and new technologies:**
elists@oreilly.com

**For technical questions about book content:**
booktech@oreilly.com

**To submit new book proposals to our editors:**
proposals@oreilly.com

**O'Reilly books are available in multiple DRM-free ebook formats. For more information:**
oreilly.com/ebooks

Lightning Source UK Ltd.
Milton Keynes UK
UKOW04f0619030317
295745UK00003B/3/P